Toward a New Catholic Church

Toward a New Catholic Church

The Promise of Reform

JAMES CARROLL

A MARINER BOOK
Houghton Mifflin Company
BOSTON   NEW YORK
2002

For information about permission to reproduce selections
from this book, write to Permissions, Houghton Mifflin Company,
215 Park Avenue South, New York, New York 10003.

Visit our Web site: www.houghtonmifflinbooks.com.

Library of Congress Cataloging-in-Publication Data
Carroll, James, date.
Toward a new Catholic Church : the promise
of reform / James Carroll.
p.   cm.
Includes bibliographical references.
ISBN 0-618-31337-0
1. Catholic Church — Doctrines. I. Title.
BX1751.3 .C37   2002
282'.09'0511—dc21
2002027262

Printed in the United States of America
QUM 10 9 8 7 6 5 4 3 2 1

Author's Note

Parts of chapter one appeared, in somewhat different form, in the *Boston Globe* and
Daedalus. Material from chapters one through six is adapted from my book *Constantine's Sword*. I gratefully acknowledge my editors: Renée Loth, Robert Turner, and Marjorie Pritchard at the *Globe;* James Miller at *Daedalus;* Wendy Strothman, Eric Chinski, and Larry Cooper at Houghton Mifflin. And loving thanks to Alexandra Marshall, my wife, who encouraged this project from the start.

For Daniel Berrigan, S.J.
and for James Parks Morton

It is not that the Gospel has changed: it is that we have begun to understand it better . . . and know that the moment has come to discern the signs of the times, to seize the opportunity and to look far ahead.

—John XXIII

Contents

Toward a New Catholic Church

1

What Is to Be Done?

I T WAS January of 2001 when I published *Constantine's Sword: The Church and the Jews,* but the twenty-first century had not really begun. Politics and religion were central to that book's consideration of Christian antisemitism, but the meaning of politics and religion both were transformed by the event that marked the new era's true beginning, which was, of course, September 11. A savage act of violence was committed in the name of Allah. America's consequent War on Terrorism, inadvertently labeled a "crusade" by President George W. Bush, is being waged with a good-versus-evil religious fervor. As with Bush, absolutism has newly gripped world leaders, especially in the tinderboxes of the Middle East, on the Indian subcontinent, and in central Asia. Challenged by these unsettling developments, religious people everywhere have undertaken an urgent new examination of the relationship between variously held beliefs and their effects on those who do not share them.

We Americans have discovered with something approaching astonishment the wild diversity of religious and spiritual impulses that has come to mark not only the planet but our own nation. "Today," as the great Catholic theologian Karl Rahner put it, "everyone is the next-door neighbor and spiritual neighbor of everyone else in the world."[1] And as Rahner argues, even from within Catholicism, this new circumstance means the assumptions of every religion must now be the subject of reexamination.

Ideological and religious elbow-rubbing is a global phenomenon, but it occurs in the United States as nowhere else. As a nation that welcomes an unending stream of immigrants, with their plethora of faiths and traditions, America implicitly sponsors this reexamination, as religiously diverse peoples encounter each other in the mundane "neighborhoods" of work, school, and living. The testing of assumptions that inevitably follows is one of the reasons America is suspect in the eyes of rigidly traditional societies.

After September 11, the Islamic presence in America drew particular attention, and the still dominant assumption of the mainly Christian, or "Judeo-Christian," character of the nation was punctured. Americans discovered that there were more Muslims living among them than Presbyterians or Episcopalians, and as many Muslims as Jews.[2] Suddenly, with Islam, on one side, being perceived as a religion that sponsors violence, and with God, on the other, being invoked as "blessing" America's War on Terrorism, religious differences as such loomed as flashpoints in the nation's life.

Meanwhile, across the globe, fundamentalist truth-claims, rooted in various religions, were seen to be fueling conflicts with ferocious new energy. In the Arab world, and in Europe, there was a virulent outbreak of the old scourge of antisemitism, with some Muslims believing that the September 11 atrocities were the work of Jews, and with some in the West inclined to accept Osama bin Laden's deadly equation between the existence of Israel and the misery of impoverished Arabs. Ariel Sharon, meanwhile, surfaced as an antisemite's dream, with few of his critics seeing his "overwhelming force" escalations against the Palestinians in the context of America's sanctioning. After all, "overwhelming force" was the mode of America's war in Afghanistan, the full costs of which have yet to be tallied. Likewise, Israel's critics have painted with the old broad brush, drawing few distinctions between the Israeli government's belligerence and the segments of Israeli society that continued to support the ideal of peace. Some drew moral equivalence between the Israel Defense Forces and Hamas, or condemned IDF incursions into Bethlehem, for example, while saying nothing about a Seder massacre in Jerusalem. Once again a stereotyped and univocal fantasy of "the Jews" was broadly seen as a problem to the world.

Hannah Arendt, the Jewish political philosopher of the mid-twentieth century, warned of the doom that follows from the idea of "eternal antisemitism," as if Jews were fated to play the victim's role. As the War on Terrorism unfolded, some reduced all of Islam to the idea of an "eternal jihad," as if the "clash of civilizations," in Samuel Huntington's phrase, between Islam and the rest of the world were inevitable. As bigoted stereotypes of Jews and their religion once more entered the common discourse, wildly distorted characterizations of Muslim belief and practice were accepted as fact. The religions of both groups were understood as motivating behavior, whether approved or condemned, that had grave consequences for humanity.

All at once, the widely held twentieth-century assumption that religion would grow increasingly irrelevant seemed naïve. The centrality of religion to life on earth, for better and for worse, had made itself very clear in a very short time. Yet never had the dark side of religion seemed more manifest, with various forms of what must be termed religious fascism being recognized as such. The Muslim suicide-murderers, wreaking such havoc in Israel, are religious fascists, certainly, but in hindsight it could be seen that so were the Catholic and Protestant fanatics of the die-hard fringes in Northern Ireland. The Hindu who assassinated Indira Gandhi was a religious fascist, and so was the Jewish student who murdered Yitzhak Rabin. What territorial compromise is possible among people who believe their claim to disputed land derives from God? What truce can interrupt violence that is held to be sacred, even if it is suicidal? Regarded across time, what religion seems free of such demonic impulses?

With numerous mainstream religions being challenged from within by their own fundamentalist extremists, and with expressly fundamentalist denominations ascendant over much of the world, the task of renewing the rational element in religion, historically minded and ecumenically disposed, has become more and more important. The capacity of each religion to engage in self-criticism and -correction has come to be seen as a compelling issue not only for the religions but for their neighbors, whose very lives may be put at risk. "There will be no peace among the nations," as the Swiss Catholic theologian Hans Küng put it, "without peace among the religions. There will be no peace among the religions without dialogue between the religions. There will be no dialogue between the religions without the investigation of the foundations of the religions."[3]

How do we correct the foundations of our beliefs when they show themselves to be inhuman? And how can basic change in religious affirmation be made without undermining the authority of the tradition itself? These are grave questions, because in an era of terrifyingly rapid change, religion functions for many people as the only connection with tradition, and it can seem desperately important to wall off the realm of faith from the chaos and uncertainty that plague everything else. But history breaks down such walls. As demonstrated by the world's move to the brink of nuclear war between Pakistan and India in the spring of 2002 in a dispute that defined itself religiously, nothing less than the future of the human race is at stake in our readiness to think critically about what we believe.

As if all of this were not enough, the Roman Catholic Church was then hit by a tidal wave that, while very different from the September catastrophe, has been for Catholics a comparable trauma. The Church has been staggered in ways no one could ever have anticipated, even in that staggering season. A few months after September 11, in early January 2002, the *Boston Globe* published a front-page story entitled "Church Allowed Abuse by Priest for Years."[4] It was an account of how Boston's archbishop, Cardinal Bernard Law, and his predecessors had protected pedophile priests, enabling them to continue what was widely characterized as their predatory crime spree against children. The scandal led to an unprecedented explosion of Catholic awareness of Church failures, and the new climate of religious self-criticism has taken on a particularly pointed meaning among Catholics, especially lay people.

An abused child had finally told his story to his mother, explaining the delay in his report by saying, "We couldn't tell you because Father said it was a confessional."[5] That statement offers a clue to the dimensions of the tragedy that broke over the Church — not only the betrayal by some priests, but the corruption of something sacred that made the revelations exponentially more shocking. In abusing their child victims, and in then controlling them, priests invoked sacraments, their own exalted status, the cult of sacred secrecy, and the wrath of God. In addition to all else, their assaults were acts of blasphemy. And when, extending this *magnum silencium,* priest-protecting bishops equated confidential out-of-court settlements with the seal of the confessional, the blasphemy became sacrilege.

Here is a shameful example: A victim named Tom Blanchette encountered Cardinal Law at the funeral of Father Joseph Birmingham. When Blanchette described to Law the way Birmingham had abused him as a child, Law, as Blanchette recounts it, "laid his hands on my head for two or three minutes. And then he said this, 'I bind you by the power of the confessional never to speak about this to anyone else.'"[6]

Child sexual abuse is by no means unique to the Catholic priesthood, but children abused by priests, in Boston and elsewhere, were typically abused twice: once by the physical assault, and then by the deflection and denial tied to the holy powers of the priesthood and the needs of the clerical culture around it. Priests raped children, and their bishops protected the priests, allowing rape to happen again. And much of this occurred in the name of God.

The scandal in Boston soon spread across the United States, as hundreds of previously undisclosed cases of fondling and rape came to light, as well as dozens of instances in which bishops exhibited more concern for the clerical institution, or even for the abusive priests, than for the traumatized victims. The cascade of revelations concerning everything from how Church personnel matters were handled to how Church funds were administered revealed that a vast anomie had gripped Catholicism. An unaddressed disorder infected clergy and laity alike, and, more broadly, Catholic attitudes toward authority—and toward gender and sexuality.

It would be simplistic to attribute the moral paralysis that so long marked Church responses to priestly child abuse to any one characteristic of Catholic culture, be it celibacy, the all-male priesthood, a Jansenist suspicion of sexuality that breeds repression, a male fear of females, or the disparity between increasingly self-respecting homosexuals in the Catholic clergy and a Catholic moral theology that continues to preach contempt for homosexuality. But taken together, such notes of contemporary Catholic conflict are indications of the dysfunction that results when the gap between preached ideals and life as it is really lived becomes too wide—especially if the ideals are false.

The Second Vatican Council (1962–1965) was the Church's great attempt to deal more honestly with the contradiction between a religious culture still firmly rooted in the Middle Ages and a Catholic people who had come of age in the modern world. Catholic attitudes toward liturgy and theology dramatically shifted. Interreligious dialogue advanced among Christians and between Christians and Jews. The Church questioned its own exercise of power. Pope John XXIII (1958–1963) trusted his fellow bishops and the Catholic people to help bring about such basic changes, but his successor, Pope Paul VI (1963–1978), made a momentous—and, history suggests, disastrous—decision to reserve two great questions to himself, trusting no one. The questions concerned birth control and priestly celibacy. In both cases the pope later handed down absolute decisions—against birth control (*Humanae Vitae*, 1968) and for celibacy (*Sacerdotalis Caelibatus*, 1967). As noted by numerous critics, and as experienced by a whole generation of Church faithful, these pronouncements led to a tragic Catholic decline.

Loyal Catholics, faced with the sex abuse scandal, want to defend the many good priests who are men of impressive virtue, yet it is these very priests who carry the burdens of dishonesty and collapse caused by those two Church policies. Catholics simply do not believe that birth control is evil, nor, from all reports, do most priests; yet the rule stands. A related "idealism" has cost the Church its credibility on all matters of sexual morality, from the so-called evils of masturbation to the rejection of condoms even when used to prevent HIV infection. Catholic leaders will oppose contraception even if it means a rise in abortion rates. To protect the ideal of marriage-for-life, priests are expected to encourage women to stay married to men who beat them. The Catholic lie about divorce is enshrined in the word "annulment." Regarding sex generally, a Catholic culture of dishonesty reigns.[7] And the bishops' inability to teach with authority on these questions is tied to a general decline in their moral influence, so that on a matter like the death penalty even a traditional Catholic like Supreme Court Justice Antonin Scalia, a death penalty advocate, can dismiss the bishops' teaching with contempt.[8]

This loss of credibility is destroying the very structure of the Church. Catholics have watched the priesthood collapse around the harried men who still serve — while the Vatican rejects the service of married men and, most disturbingly, refuses to ordain women, on the strictly fundamentalist ground that all of the apostles were male. The Vatican has said its pronouncement against women priests is forever and infallible, yet most Catholics reject it. Meanwhile, more than half the parishes in the world have no priest, and what priests remain are aging fast. Why this crisis? Because virginal sexlessness is deemed morally superior to an actively erotic life—an inhuman idea that opens a gap, an ethical abyss, into which the most well meaning of people can fall.

None of these factors, taken alone, led to the sexual abuse of children by priests, but when that horrible crime occurs, the culture of silence, denial, dishonesty, and collapse makes it far less likely that the Church, from the hierarchy to the people in the pew, will respond honestly and wisely. That is why the scandal must lead to more than accusations and the disciplining of individuals. The abusers punished and removed, yes. The bishops repentant and held accountable, yes. The children protected above all. But the scandal must also lead to a new awareness of what it means to be Catholic—no longer at the mercy of the moral paralysis of Church leaders or the corruptions they defend. This is why the Catholic people, whose instinctive response to the abuse crisis has been clear from that traumatic January forward, moved at once to take the Church back. Using every forum they could, Catholics began demanding reform—for the sake of their beloved Church and, more important, for the sake of the children.

In parishes throughout the United States, Catholics gathered in large numbers to discuss a range of matters spilling over from the abuse crisis. As reports surfaced of financial settlements secretly paid to victims over the years, Catholic philanthropists and foundations demanded an accounting of the monies they donated to the Church,[9] and parishioners began withholding contributions from collection baskets. One lay group, Voice of the Faithful, founded at St. John the Evangelist Church in Wellesley, Massachusetts, soon had fourteen thousand Catholics enrolled in its cause, which was defined by the slogan "Keep the faith, change the Church."[10] Even conservative Catholics, in rejecting the passive role traditionally assigned by the hierarchy to lay people, found themselves enlisted, perhaps despite themselves, in what the *New York Times* called "a quiet revolution."[11]

My preoccupation in *Constantine's Sword* was with the history of Christian antisemitism and how this primordial sin of the Church had prepared the ground out of which grew the Nazi program to eliminate the Jewish people. Recognitions tied to the Holocaust led to a massive postwar Christian reform, nowhere more profound than in the Roman Catholic Church. But the Church reforms begun at Vatican II were not sustained, in part because Church authorities began to roll them back, as we saw with Paul VI's encyclicals, and in part because the Catholic laity, despite its implicit dissent on those and other matters, was never able to take the practical responsibility for the Church that the council had made theoretically possible. And under the pontificate of the charismatic and admired John Paul II, the laity, with some vocal but always marginal exceptions, seemed happy to resume its traditional role as adjunct to "the Church," which continued to define itself as, essentially, the priests, the bishops, and the pope.

In fact, defining the Church as "the People of God," Vatican II had established the principles to which the new lay-dominated grassroots movement of change instinctively appealed in the wake of the abuse scandal. The tragic irony, of course, was that what the Holocaust had proven unable to do — spark a sustained awareness of the need for Church reform among Catholics — the priest sex scandal showed every sign of doing.

This can reflect badly on Catholics, but it can also indicate the kind of power that is generated when a large moral problem is joined to the self-interest of the news industry. If the Holocaust never fully cracked open the Christian conscience, it also never gripped the media like a story involving sex and the disgrace of admired figures.

The Catholic Church, proven incapable of protecting its most vulnerable members, has been humiliated in the twenty-first century in ways that—despite its grievous failures in the past, notably its failure in relation to the Jewish people—it was not humiliated in the twentieth. Pope Pius XII, after all, may yet be named a saint. The Church failed in the face of Hitler's Final Solution because Jews never fully belonged within the circle of Catholic concern. But who occupies the very center of that circle if not Catholic children? This Church, indeed, has organized itself around its children, and this fact, too, fuels the scandal. The shock is that both the pederast priests and the institution-protecting bishops betrayed *them*.

Still, the revelation here repeats what was brought into the open by the Holocaust: the plain fact of the sinfulness of a Church that prefers to think of itself as the sinless "Bride of Christ."[12] Indeed, that wish to be understood as above the human condition, as an organization existentially incapable of sin, is part of what caused the Church to fail in both cases. Catholics have deflected the real meaning of Christian anti-semitism, and have only partially dismantled the dogma and theology that led to it, for the same reason that bishops could not bring themselves to face the full meaning of priestly child abuse. "Sinful members" of the Church caused antisemitism, in this view, as "wayward priests" (and perhaps an "obsessive media") caused the abuse scandal. Few Catholics would any longer define the Church as the "perfect society," as popes once did, but Rome still insists on the moral perfection of "the Church as such," an assertion to which we will return in the next chapter. If transgressions occur, they are always the result of the aberrant behavior of individuals—perhaps including individual priests, bishops, or even a pope—but never of the institutional, theological, or dogmatic aspects of Catholicism.

And so the scaffolding of denial was firmly in place in January 2002 when the scandal broke. Priests are *alter Christi,* and whatever their private flaws, they simply cannot be publicly found guilty of grievous sin. Gospel texts are inspired by the Holy Spirit, so even if they slander the religion of Israel, these texts simply have nothing to do with antisemitism. The Church is simply incapable of mistakes in matters of "faith and morals." The pinnacle of such an assertion, the symbol of it, is the dogma of papal infallibility. That dogma, formally dating only to 1870, is narrowly applied, but its aura infects the exercise of authority throughout the Church. We will see more of it later.

It is out of this conviction of Catholic exceptionalism that Church leaders, when faced with obvious failure, whether the "silence" of Pius XII in the face of genocide or the abuse of children by priests, put such a priority on avoiding scandal, which really means covering up anything that might call the sinlessness of the "Church as such" into question. If sins are nevertheless exposed, they are blamed on the members, leaving the blameless Church with no reason to change.

An authentic reading of the history of the Church's failure before and during the Holocaust, like any reading of the current Church failure of children, blows this fantasy away. And there lies the hope. The Church, too, is mortal. The Church is not divine. If the Church is the "Bride of Christ," it is the unfaithful spouse of whom Hosea speaks[13]—an image not of human faithfulness, but of God's. The wonder of biblical faith, what Christians call the Good News, is that God has chosen human instruments as a way to be present in history. Our humanity is the point. When we pretend to be angels, we are not only committing the classically defined sin of pride, we are dangerous. It is not incidental to the present crisis of the priesthood that such angelic thinking involves an inhuman repressiveness when it comes to sexuality. That, too, is dangerous.

Until now, the Church has treated its own humanity like a dirty secret, yet it should be the opposite of that. If the Church were less conflicted about its limits, it could deal with its failures more forthrightly, with an eye to something besides avoiding scandal. This would mean, after the Holocaust and after priestly child abuse, that the elimination of antisemitism and the protection of children would be given the highest priority. In both cases, real reform would follow.

But that presumes a change not only in the way bishops and popes regard the Church, but in how the Catholic people do, and here the lesson of a seemingly minor change in the way we attend Mass is instructive. It used to be that those approaching the communion rail would kneel and, with head tilted back and mouth open, offer their tongues onto which the priest—only the priest—would place a consecrated wafer. Catholics never gave this procedure a thought until, with the reforms of Vatican II in the late 1960s, it changed. No more kneeling. No more outstretched tongues. No more communion rail, even: what had been an effective barrier between sanctuary and church was removed. Now lay people as well as priests distribute communion. Now Catholics receive the sacred bread in their hands and place it in their mouths themselves.

This subtle reform has tremendous significance, for it means that Catholics no longer take the sacrament in a feeding gesture appropriate only to small children. The subservient kneeling is gone, marking members of this community as being of equal standing. Every Christian, not just the ordained, is worthy to handle the Body of Christ. The hierarchy of virtue, with some assumed to be more worthy than others, is gone.

These changes symbolize a mature Church whose members are treated as fully of age, but alas, the Catholic Church is not really like that yet. When the further reforms of Vatican II were stymied by a reactionary pope and his conforming bishops, the infantilizing culture of Catholicism survived. Such Church leaders love to speak of the Church as a family but always assume that they are the parents— "Father"— and everyone else is a child. One of the reasons Catholics are so shocked by the betrayals of priests and bishops is that Catholics continued to regard them, as children do parents, as morally superior people. That they are not comes as a big surprise. "Father" is mortal too.

In fact, Catholics who have come so fully of age in other ways remain religiously immature. They may be superbly educated in a range of disciplines, but they tend to be theologically illiterate. They may be presidents of universities and corporations, but in church lay people still do little more than take up the collection or arrange the flowers. And when they have dared diverge from the paternalistic hierarchy, making their own decisions about birth control, for example, Catholics have done so in the manner of adolescents, defying authority slyly rather than openly. In the face of the criminal Vatican rejection of condoms for HIV prevention, Catholics have been passive instead of outraged. That Catholics seeking divorce willingly undergo the humiliations and lies of the annulment system is another signal of immaturity. By submitting to the paternalistic Church structure, otherwise adult Catholics have allowed the culture of Church dishonesty to worsen to the point of the present pathology. We all share responsibility for this catastrophe.

But the present crisis makes it impossible for Catholics to continue this childish arrangement. Once the myth of the perfect parent is broken, the young can grow into adulthood, taking responsibility for themselves. Catholics can never regard priests and bishops uncritically again, nor can they cooperate any longer in the small dishonesties that have spawned such massive betrayal. Now when Catholics go to Mass, the symbols of maturity and equality already in place must be matched with new political structures, which means that the most ecclesiastically incorrect word of all must at last be spoken aloud. The next time someone announces that the Church is not a democracy, the reply should be that that is precisely the problem. Checks and balances, due process, open procedures, elections, a fully educated community, freedom of conscience, the right to dissent, authority as service instead of as domination, moral leadership by rational explanation instead of by assertion — all of this must come into the Church, and later in this book we will see why.

Here is the lesson: a power structure that is accountable only to itself will always end by abusing the powerless. Even then, it will paternalistically ask to be trusted to repair the damage. Never again. Not only the discredited bishops who protected abusive priests must go; the whole system that produced them must go. Full democratic reform is the Catholic Church's only hope. If we can take the Body of Christ in hand, we can take the Church in hand too.

But is a genuine — and necessarily radical — reform of the Roman Catholic Church really possible?

I am inclined to answer that question with other questions:

Who would have thought that real reform of the Soviet Union was possible? But a grassroots movement, beginning with an unknown electrician in a Gdańsk shipyard, made it so. Who would have thought real reform of the brutal apartheid regime in South Africa was possible? But a grassroots movement led from an island cell by a state-demonized prisoner made it so. In the United States, grassroots movements changed the legal and social status of black people, and a grassroots movement stopped the Pentagon's escalations of the Vietnam War. Around the world, grassroots movements of women and girls, whether identifying as feminists or not, are changing institutions and societies, even the most repressive of them. And it is far from incidental to the project of Catholic reform that a grassroots organization that played a crucial role in ending the arms race—the joint Soviet-American International Physicians for the Prevention of Nuclear War, which won the Nobel Peace Prize in 1985—was cofounded by Dr. James Muller, who was also a founder, in 2001 at St. John the Evangelist in Wellesley, of Voice of the Faithful, the grassroots organization of lay Catholics already mentioned. The Catholic Church is a command society, but it is neither a brutal dictatorship nor an apartheid regime, and once the Catholic people fully assert themselves, real reform will follow.

Returning to the historic challenge facing all religions after September 11, we begin to see why the struggle within Roman Catholicism matters so much. Every Catholic has intensely personal reasons for wanting a renewed Catholicism: the consolation of the sacraments, the access to transcendence, the healing memory of Jesus Christ made present, a way to imagine life after death. But Catholics also see that the stakes for Church renewal are far greater than the merely personal. At a time when the global gap between rich and poor widens every year—the very precondition of terrorism—will the Catholic Church survive as one of the few institutions that inherently bridges that gap? Will the Church sustain its traditional role as a defender of the poor and its more contemporary function as a rare critic of free-market capitalism? In the twentieth century, the Catholic Church in Europe, and even more in the United States, overcame its ancient affiliation with wealth to become a friend of labor; in the developing world, often despite the Vatican, the Church has been on the side of liberation. Its image as a bulwark of social conservation, in other words, is only partly accurate. The Church has also been a force for progressive social change. Will it continue to be? Or, like other religions, will it, too, emphasize spiritual beatitude over the passion for justice?

As mindless superstition encroaches on every religion, and as new-age banalities increasingly satisfy the human need for a language of transcendence, will the Catholic intellectual tradition, which gave rise to universities and even to scientific rationalism, survive as more than a side chapel of nostalgia in an otherwise enthusiastic Church? With scientific rationalism itself exposed by the twentieth century as an inadequate source of meaning, can Catholic thought contribute to *its* correction? Or will Catholicism follow major components of world Protestantism into the cul-de-sac of fundamentalism? Will biblical scholarship and historical criticism of theology, and the related capacity for correcting dogma, move from the margins of Catholic academia into the parishes, or only into the past? Will the Catholic prejudice against violence, embodied in John XXIII's *Pacem in Terris* and in John Paul II's opposition to war, including wars waged by America, be lost to a world increasingly on a hair trigger? The September 11 catastrophe has shown how religious impulses can be perverted into sectarian fanaticism, resulting in violent horrors. Respectful exchange between religions, and correction within them, are now preconditions of world peace. Can the shaken Catholic Church rise to this challenge?

It is too soon to know the answer to these questions. But to put my own conviction plainly: the twenty-first century desperately needs an intellectually vital, ecumenically open, and morally sound Catholicism, a Catholicism fully itself—that is, a Catholicism profoundly reformed. The world needs a new Catholic Church.

It is with such stakes in mind that I have returned in this book to "A Call for Vatican III," with which I concluded the long history of the relations between Catholics and Jews in *Constantine's Sword*. An unyielding look at the tragic and wicked tradition of sacred hatred of Jews brought to the surface numerous problems in Church belief and practice that have still not been completely confronted. Those problems run deep in the Catholic character, with dread consequences for more than Jewish-Christian relations. The chapters that follow, adapted from "A Call for Vatican III," lay out the elements of reform that seemed essential if antisemitism were to be left behind, but here I elaborate and adjust those elements in light of the new crises of religion in general and Catholicism in particular.

The priest sex abuse scandal is a Catholic catastrophe. That word in Greek means reversal or turning point. In Hebrew it is rendered as *shoah*. A catastrophe, classically defined in the literature of tragedy, is the occasion on which humans are finally able to see the truth of what is wrong in their lives, and thereby to see what must happen to reverse what is wrong and make it right. That is the genius of the human capacity for change, and it is the promise of reform. In seeing how reform is necessary, we will see how it is possible.

This terrible time, in which awful sins of the Catholic Church have been clearly laid bare, can be the start of the Church's great renewal. Therefore, despite our heartbreak, anger, and fear, we say, as biblical people have always said, "Praised be thou, Lord our God, King of the Universe, who has allowed us to live to see this day."[14]

2

The Broad Relevance
of Catholic Reform

I WAS NINETEEN years old when the Second Vatican
Council convened in 1962. I had recently entered the seminary, and for the next seven years my coming fully into
Catholic adulthood, and to the priesthood itself in 1969,
would be shaped by that magnificent *aggiornamento*, as Pope
John XXIII called it. Even now, on the cusp of old age, I remain
a child of Vatican II, and this book will show why.

At the time, I thought that the greatest significance of the reforming council was its concern with various aspects of internal
Catholic renewal, but looking back on the broad social change
that marked the last third of the twentieth century, beginning in
the 1960s, I see the council's significance for an entire society
beyond the Church. Even among non-Catholics, for example,
the figure of Pope John is linked in memory with that of John
Kennedy, and for good reason. Pope John's program of reform
within the Church helped stimulate the transformation of cultural attitudes that swept Europe and the United States in the
sixties. The liberalization of Catholic theology reflected that social mutation and advanced it, and that process is not complete.
As the forces of religion have become, by the early twenty-first

century, ever more fundamentalist, yoked to political reaction and ethnic chauvinism, and as scientific rationalism has proven to be a woefully incomplete ideology, there is, to repeat, more need than ever for a revived Catholicism committed to intellectual rigor, open inquiry, and respect for the other. To use a past Vatican Council that began to revitalize and humanize the Church as a model of what a future council can be is to put the prospect of progressive societal change before a wide audience. In nothing is this more true than in relation to the task of ending antisemitism forever, which was the urgent purpose of *Constantine's Sword*. But the events of September 11 and the Catholic sex scandal both suggest how other urgent questions, from religious violence to the protection of children, are tied to the task of Catholic reform.

It is important to keep the long view in mind. The Second Vatican Council represented the beginning of the long-overdue demise of a Constantinian imperial Catholicism. Patriarchy as the dominant mode of organization, intolerance of internal dissent (heresy), and contempt for other religions (especially Judaism) took hold of the Catholic imagination by the fifth century as never before, and the hold continues. During the Middle Ages, sacred power was concentrated in a papacy that understood itself as an absolute monarchy. When all of this was challenged by the Protestant Reformation, the Catholic Church responded, perhaps understandably, with a defensiveness and rigidity that peaked in the Church's war against modernity. The nineteenth century showed the Church in desperate revolt against a rapidly changing world. This tragic dynamic was ended by Vatican II, which was, at bottom, the Church's declaration of truce, not only with outsiders but with itself.

By the time I wrote *Constantine's Sword*, I understood that improving the Church's relations with Jews was not merely one agenda item among others. Of course there *were* others: the rights of women, the end of patriarchal autocracy, the restoration of simple honesty, the recovery from clericalism, the place of the laity, the abandonment of denominational narcissism in relation to other churches, an affirmation of sexuality—not to mention my hope as a young priest for the right to marry. Because antisemitism had been a defining ideology of Christianity from early on, dismantling its theological structure, as began to happen in the momentous 1965 declaration *Nostra Aetate,* was a signal council task, but even this preeminent reform is tied to all the others. A Church that renounces contempt for Jews is on the way to renouncing its triumphalist condescension toward other believers—and today that emphatically must include Islam—as well as its intolerance for its own dissenters. The Jew as the paradigmatic "hated other" can be the avatar of liberation for all the "others" who have been subjected to Constantinian oppressiveness. To dismantle one pillar of the imperial autocracy is to dismantle them all.

As a young man, I consciously defined a first ideal for myself in terms of the Church into which I was born. When I entered the Paulist Fathers' novitiate in 1962, I lived according to a daily schedule that had been set by the Council of Trent in the sixteenth century, observing rubrics of contemplation, scholasticism, and manual labor that preserved a puritanical regimen. And I loved it. But also, equally consciously, I had been drawn to that life by my brush with Pope John XXIII, who had taken me in his arms.

As I have written elsewhere, my father was a senior American military officer in Europe in 1959, and our family was honored with a private audience with the pope. I was a sixteen-year-old boy, but I towered above him, and bent to accept his embrace. I never forgot his red velvet shoe next to my penny loafer, the soapy aroma of his shaven face, his whiskers scraping my cheek. The curl of the words he whispered remained in my ear; their intimate affection had conscripted me, though I did not understand what he had said. What drew me to him, to the Church, and to what I thought of as God was the clear fact of Pope John's being anything but a puritan.[1]

The world loved him so, and I did, simply because he was not a misanthrope. No Catholic would have admitted it, but the Church, with its Constantinian legacy, was institutionalized and bureaucratized misanthropy itself.[2] We took the weight of its world hatred so much for granted that a life-loving man like Pope John could seem a miraculous exception. He was not interested in being a museum keeper, he said. Instead, he wanted "to cultivate a flourishing garden of life."[3] The enthusiasm with which the Church, and those outside it, took to him was itself a grievous, if implicit, indictment of what we Catholics had allowed ourselves to become.

This was the pope who left for others the question of infallibility, declaring that he, for one, would never speak infallibly.[4] He was given to spontaneous remarks and jokes at his own expense. He disliked the pomp of office. To avoid being cheered like a potentate as he entered St. Peter's Basilica, he ordered the choirmaster to lead the throng in singing. When he visited the Regina Coeli prison in Rome, his biographer Peter Hebblethwaite wrote, he eschewed the condescending piety that usually marks such encounters and quietly told the inmates of his own uncle who had served time. In the middle of the Cuban missile crisis, in October 1962, he addressed an unprecedented message to the leaders of the United States, the Soviet Union, and the rest of the world. His words were reported the next day on the front page of *Pravda*, in Moscow, under the headline "We Beg All Rulers Not to Be Deaf to the Cry of Humanity." "This was unheard of," Hebblethwaite commented. "John's appeal enabled Nikita Khrushchev, the Soviet leader, to back down without losing face."[5] Only months later, in his encyclical *Pacem in Terris*, he broke with Cold War orthodoxy and raised the question of whether nuclear weapons could ever be used as an instrument of justice, sowing the seeds of a new Catholic conscientious objection. John XXIII did not initiate the peace movement of the 1960s, but his anticipation of it would serve as a powerful inspiration. Similarly with détente, for he embraced the nephew of Khrushchev at a time when other Western leaders were still demonizing Communists. Equally significant, he was one of the first to recognize the coming power of the women's movement, which he flagged, together with the demise of colonialism and the rise of workers, as one of the welcome signs of the times. "Since women are becoming ever more conscious of their dignity," he wrote, "they will not tolerate being treated as mere material instruments, but demand rights befitting a human person both in domestic and in public life."[6]

John XXIII's pontificate was marked by that sort of prophetic insight, but equally marked by the steady work of practical change within the institution over which he presided. When he issued his surprising summons to the Vatican Council, barely six months after being elected, he said it was not for the purpose of condemning errors. The world didn't need the Church for that, he said, for "nowadays men are condemning them of their own accord."[7] When, at the beginning of Vatican II, he denounced the "prophets of doom," everyone knew that he was speaking of those who had set the tone in his own Church for generations. He was himself an alternative example of what the Church could now become. "As unforgettable as his person was," Hans Küng wrote of Pope John, "what he achieved for the Catholic Church was unforgettable too. In five years he renewed the Catholic Church more than his predecessors had in five hundred years . . . Only with John did the Middle Ages come to an end in the Catholic Church."[8]

Decades later, after my long study of Christian antisemitism and after the traumas of 2001 and 2002, I see all this in the context of the intersections of religion and politics, belief and violence. In nothing are those intersections made more vivid than in the Holocaust.

Angelo Giuseppe Roncalli was just turning seventy-seven when he assumed the papacy in 1958, elected as a compromise candidate whose great age was expected to keep him from doing much as pope. For the previous six years he had been the archbishop of Venice, but for the quarter century before that he had served as a Vatican diplomat in Bulgaria, Turkey, and France. The dominant experience he had had as a priest was of the devastation of World War II. He saw it not from the perspective of the sacristy, nor of Vatican City, but of ruined cities, refugee centers, the camps. Roncalli was one of the only Catholic prelates in Europe who, as a legate in Bulgaria and in Turkey providing counterfeit baptismal records for thousands of fugitive Jews, had actively resisted the Holocaust.[9] In this regard, there is sharp relevance in an anecdote related by Hannah Arendt about Rolf Hochhuth's *The Deputy,* first produced in 1963. The play offered a devastating portrait of Pius XII's "silence" during the Holocaust. When asked what should be done against the play, Arendt reported, Pope John allegedly replied, "Do against it? What can you do against the truth?"[10]

The Church's failure in relation to Adolf Hitler was only a symptom of the ecclesiastical cancer Pope John was attempting to treat. The long tradition of Christian Jew-hatred, on which Hitler had so efficiently built, was the malignant tumor that had metastasized in the mystical body. John XXIII had instinctively grasped this. Hence his open-hearted response to the Jewish historian Jules Isaac (in June 1960), who traced the Church's antisemitism to the Gospels, and John's subsequent charge (in September) to those preparing for the Vatican Council that it take up the Church's relations with Judaism as a matter of priority. Hence his elimination from the Good Friday liturgy of the modifiers "faithless" and "perfidious" as applied to Jews, an implicit rejection of long-standing Catholic contempt for the Jewish religion.[11] Hence his greeting to a first Jewish delegation at the Vatican: "I am Joseph, your brother," he said, then came down from his throne to sit with them in a simple chair.[12] To appreciate this gesture, one need only think of the "pope's Jews" kissing the ground trod by the velvet slipper before returning to their "hole," as Pius IX, speaking not long before Roncalli was born, had called the ghetto at the foot of Vatican Hill.

For hundreds of years, popes had defined their power in terms of their sovereignty over Jews, and while the ill effects of that power were also felt by women, by those defined as heretics, and by Muslims, who since the eighth century had been Christendom's hated, outside other, Jews were the "intimate enemy." Antisemitism always had a kind of primal status as the Church's first, and permanent, mistake—an unbroken chain of choice and consequence that crossed the centuries. For nearly two thousand years Catholic theology had projected almost every affirmation of the Church against the negative screen of a detested Judaism. That narrative refutes the core idea, expressed in various ways, that the Church is a "perfect society," that as the Bride of Christ it is spotless, that the claim to infallibility in matters of faith and morals is more than wishful thinking or rank denial. It is not too much to assume that for John XXIII the Holocaust, which he saw up close and experienced as a trauma of his own, exposed this deeply entrenched assumption to profound questioning.

At bottom, what was so urgently required of the Catholic Church was a change in what it said, thought, and believed about Jews. A reform that addressed the problem of Catholic antisemitism could be anything but peripheral, and the Church's relations with Jews could be anything but just one more item on the council's agenda. This was so not only because the ongoing faith of Jews called into question absolutist claims made for Jesus Christ, not only because steady Jewish affirmation of the Shema apparently contradicted the principal tenets of the Christian creed, and not only because the universalist exclusivism of the Catholic Church was incompatible with authentic respect for Israel's unbroken covenant with God. The council's mandate to reform the Church was rooted in the history of its relations with Jews because that history, more than anything else, established the Church's radical sinfulness. And Pope John saw it. That the Church needed reform in other ways took nothing from this core question. Indeed, since the Holocaust was the event laying bare the Church's complicity with evil, this recognition is exactly what led to awareness of the need for sweeping change.

Pope John died of stomach cancer in June 1963, not long after the promulgation of *Pacem in Terris* and after presiding at the first session of Vatican II. There would be three more sessions, presided over by Pope Paul VI. As Giovanni Battista Montini, he had worked as a devoted factotum to Pius XII, and that background showed in his pontificate. Pressed to establish the "cause" of John XXIII's candidacy for sainthood, Paul VI at the same time established that of Pius XII, as if the two men were in any way comparable. Acting out of the old (but not that old) instinct of papal primacy, Paul VI undercut the council when he refused to allow its members to consider the pressing questions of priestly celibacy and birth control. Defying what could easily have been opposite outcomes if the council fathers had taken up those questions, he issued the independent encyclicals *Sacerdotalis Caelibatus* and *Humanae Vitae,* upholding the traditional requirement that priests not marry and banning contraception.

I was ordained to the priesthood within months of *Humanae Vitae,* not appreciating yet the damage that it and the other pronouncement had done. I was later one of many thousands of Catholic priests who left the priesthood once that damage became clear. The disconnect between the teachings of these encyclicals and the lives Catholics were leading was too great, and the blow that the condemnation of birth control was to Church authority and integrity is well known.[13]

Given the ideology of papal absolutism that he inherited from his mentor Pius XII, Paul VI thought he had no choice but to reaffirm teachings that had been firmly adhered to by popes for a thousand years or more. His was the first effort to turn back the tide of Church reform that the Vatican Council initiated, and that program of medieval restoration was vigorously continued by Pope John Paul II. The question of the Church's relations with Jews was the only one that the Polish pope advanced, and his contribution to Jewish-Catholic reconciliation will be remembered as the great achievement of his pontificate.

But even that is the beginning of something, not the end. I have already described as momentous the Vatican Council declaration *Nostra Aetate,* which stated that "what happened in his [Christ's] passion cannot be blamed upon all the Jews then living, without distinction, nor upon the Jews of today." However, this clear renunciation of the original "blood libel," a source of Christian antisemitism, raised as many questions as it answered. I recall that we seminarians greeted the decree with perplexity because, while *Nostra Aetate* was put forward as if it were rebutting a marginal slander of gutter antisemitism, as students of the New Testament we knew that the sacred texts of the Church placed just such blame on the Jews then living and "on [their] children."[14] We also knew that, from what we thought of as its origins, the Church had defined itself as the replacement of Judaism, and that because Judaism had refused to yield to that claim, the Church had further defined itself as the enemy of Judaism. *Nostra Aetate* took up none of this, but by defining as a lie an affirmation at the center of the Gospel, it clearly put such basic questions on the Church's near-term agenda. Indeed, *Nostra Aetate* implicitly raised the issue of whether, in its first generation, the Church had already betrayed its master.

We did not know it at the time, but *Nostra Aetate,* as promulgated by the council, was a considerably watered-down document when compared to earlier drafts. It probably fell far short of what John XXIII, responding to Jules Isaac, had wanted. For example, the first thought was that the council would make a stand-alone statement, entitled *Decretum de Judaeis,* about relations between the Church and Judaism, but *Nostra Aetate* is a declaration on all non-Christian religions, with only one small section devoted to Judaism. In the initiating spirit of Pope John, many council fathers expected the statement to include an acknowledgment of Church culpability. "Why can we not draw from the Gospel," one bishop asked during debate in the nave of St. Peter's, "the magnanimity to beg for forgiveness, in the name of so many Christians, for so many and so great injustices?"[15]

But it was not to be. *Nostra Aetate* "deplores the hatred, persecutions, and displays of anti-Semitism directed against the Jews at any time and from any source,"[16] but, of course, it seems not to know what the main source of the hatred, persecutions, and displays had been. As with the rejection of the deicide charge, the declaration here seems oddly incomplete, as if saying, We can go into this so far, but no farther. And sadly, the apology for sins against the people of Israel that Pope John Paul II offered in a momentous ceremony in St. Peter's on March 12, 2000, also avoided a direct confrontation with the source of antisemitism. We will turn to that apology's positive aspect later, but here we must note its shortfall. "We are deeply saddened," the pope prayed on that occasion, "by the behavior of those who in the course of history have caused these children of yours [Jews] to suffer." It was possible to hear that apology as regret for behavior that was inconsistent with core Church teaching, instead of set in motion by it.

In such difficult matters, any step toward authentic reckoning is to be welcomed. The papal apology in March 2000 built on what was said at the council, but honesty requires the acknowledgment that the early pattern of deflection has been continued. Here is how one historian of the council summed up what happened. "The Declaration *Nostra Aetate* had a very difficult and troubled development in the council, which recalls in many ways the tragic bimillennial history of relations between Christians and Jews and makes it seem almost miraculous that the declaration ever appeared. Indiscretions, intrigues, near-eastern misunderstandings and fears, especially of a political nature, all became entangled. In addition to this, there was what could be called 'Christian obstinacy,' a certain inability to understand, found among some Christians at the council. They were mentally unprepared for the topic."[17]

Or perhaps not. Maybe the council fathers had such difficulty because they grasped, if only subliminally, how far into the ground of theology the spike of this question goes. And perhaps that still accounts for the Church's inability to face this history more directly. The "topic" of the Jews—like the "topic" of women—has truly far-reaching implications. Neither the fathers of Vatican II nor Pope Paul VI was prepared to examine the foundational assumptions of Christian faith, the prophecy-fulfillment structure of salvation history, the construction of a Passion narrative requiring the Messiah to be rejected by "his own," and atonement Christology itself, which has Jesus saving the baptized (only the baptized) from the Jewish God, as this all implied a denigration of the Jews. Instead, acting from good intentions, Church fathers hoped to renounce the denigration, but without facing what made it inevitable.

And so with Pope John Paul II. Continuing the pattern, he seems to have assumed that heartfelt gestures of friendship toward Jews, combined with sincere sympathy for Jewish suffering and abstract acts of repentance, would suffice. When Jews seemed to say otherwise, they were slapped down for being ungrateful. And always, from discussions of Holy Week pogroms to the Inquisition to the Final Solution, there has been the commitment to keep any shadow of moral culpability or accusation of sin away from, in John Paul II's phrase, "the Church as such." Thus the 1998 "confession," "We Remember: A Reflection on the Shoah," acknowledges the failures of some of the Church's children, but not of the Church. Similarly with the subsequent declaration, "Memory and Reconciliation: The Church and the Faults of the Past," issued just before the repentance ceremony in St. Peter's. This distinction between the sins of the "members" and the purity of "the Church as such," conceived of as the sinless Bride of Christ, also undergirds the hierarchy's recent effort to condemn priest pederasts, and even, perhaps, an occasional enabling bishop, without examining the religious and institutional sources of such behavior.

The examination of conscience for which John XXIII had called at Vatican II required more than was possible at the time, probably more than even he envisaged. It is one thing to consider allowing priests to marry or couples to practice contraception—and the Church has so far proved itself incapable of doing even that—but really to eliminate existential condescension toward women, religious assumptions about the impurity of sex, not to mention the contempt for Jews that lives not in the hearts of prejudiced Christians but in the heart of "the Church as such"—all that requires fundamental changes in the way history has been written, theology has been taught, and Scripture has been interpreted. Indeed, in this context, the very character of Scripture as sacred text becomes an issue. Not even the Reformation, as traumatic as it was, sought to go this deeply into the meaning of the tradition, as is clear from Martin Luther's masterly appropriation of the tradition's antisemitism. So, yes, the reforming impulse of Vatican II fell far short of what was needed, and yes, in the years since, the authorities of the

Church have done their best to dampen any return to that impulse within Catholicism. How, given this history, could it have been otherwise?

Yet the reforming impulse refuses to die, even in the Church, because the event that set it moving has only continued to grow in force in the conscience of the West. This is what it means that, at bottom, Pope John XXIII was responding to the Holocaust. The Final Solution has refused to remain unadjudicated in institutions everywhere. If Bayer, Swiss banks, the Louvre, owners of apartments in the Eighth Arrondissement, the Ford Motor Company, the U.S. Treasury Department, and the *New York Times* are made to confront their relationship to this unfinished business of the twentieth century, so with the Catholic Church. If Argentina can repent, as its president did in June 2000, of having offered refuge to Nazi war criminals, why can't the Vatican repent of having helped some of those same war criminals escape to Argentina? As a Catholic, I have been raised with the intuition that such moral reckoning is essential to the life of conscience, whether the individual's or the community's. And political events of the early twenty-first century, with the ugly return of overt antisemitism, reinforcing the insecurity of Israel at the worst possible time, leaving many Jews to wonder if again they are on their own, have made it clear once more that this moral reckoning must be carried forward. Sacred hatred of Jews, the tradition of which the Church, despite its best intentions, is still a custodian, simply must be more fully rejected. Peace depends on it.

In reaction to the Protestant Reformation, a defensive Catholicism adopted the attitude that, sinless in itself, "the Church as such" had no need of reformation, yet that was an anomalous mistake, in violation of a much older Catholic tradition. Ironically, in rejecting the spirit of modernity, the Roman Catholic Church, with a certitude to rival that of the crassest sort of Enlightenment science, had perfectly embodied that spirit. John XXIII's greatest achievement was to declare the time over when the Church could so blithely stand as a monument of self-contradiction, if decidedly not of self-criticism. The council he called was the twenty-first "ecumenical" gathering of Church leaders, and though that means such an event had happened, on average, more than once each century, the only council that had met since the defensive Trent (1545–1563) was the hyperdefensive Vatican I (1869–1870), where papal primacy and papal infallibility were defined as dogmas. But the tradition of the councils itself was a proclamation of the Church's ongoing fallibility, its permanent need for reformation. That charged word was introduced into Church parlance not by Martin Luther but by the fathers of the Council of Constance (1414–1418), which called for "reform in faith and practice, in head and members."[18] *Ecclesia semper reformanda,* the Church forever being reformed, is another old slogan. The hope that resides in this enterprise, "firmly grounded in the Catholic tradition," is caught by Hans Küng when he points out that the Latin *reformare* means "to shape something according to its own essential being."[19]

The first General Council met at Nicaea in 325, and it was nothing but an effort to overcome disputes, factions, and fractures—notes of a community that saw itself as anything but perfect. Indeed, the Church of that era, coming under the sway of the emperor and convert Constantine, was riven by heresies —and by open displays of ferocious Jew hatred. At Nicaea, bishops agreed on the defining creed, but precisely so that Constantine could use it to impose ideological order on the empire and, not incidentally, extend his power. Subsequent councils were equally marked by the confluence of belief and politics. They were called to heal schisms, to settle feuds, and to resolve absolutely contradictory claims made absolutely. The councils always took up the business of the Church's imperfections, and they often had to respond to the imperfections of the popes. The Council of Constantinople (680–681) condemned Pope Honorius I as a heretic. The Council of Constance, when confronted with three claimants to the papacy, forced the resignation of one, deposed the other two, and elected a new pope of its own. Constance issued the proclamation *Sacrasancta*, which established the superiority of council over pope. The assumption took hold that the Church council exercised ultimate authority in the Church, and so there is something wonderfully absurd—something "modern" despite itself—about a council vesting just such authority in the figure of the pope. (How do we know that pope is above council? The council says so!)

Vatican I took its name from the place where it met, St. Peter's Basilica in the Vatican. Nearly eight hundred bishops convened, almost all Europeans (forty-eight bishops represented the United States, but many of them would have been immigrants). The council was presided over by Pope Pius IX (1846–1878), who had for twenty-five years as pope already set his face against everything associated with liberalism. There were good reasons why the Catholic Church was defining its struggle against the spirit of modernism as a fight to the death: the archbishop of Paris would soon be murdered by mobs of the Commune. The pope's authority over his own territories was being threatened by the movement of Italian nationalism, and nationalism itself was seen as incompatible with the

Church's exercise of civil and theological authority across borders. Catholic theology was perceived as being undermined by liberal ideas. Pius IX's solution to all of this was to draw from the bishops gathered in council an unprecedented affirmation of his own authority as pope, and he succeeded.

Vatican I's declaration in support of Pius was issued as the constitution *Pastor Aeternus*. "When the Roman Pontiff speaks *ex cathedra*," it said, "that is, when . . . as pastor and teacher of all Christians in virtue of his highest apostolic authority, he defines a doctrine of faith and morals that must be held by the Universal Church, he is empowered through the divine assistance promised him in blessed Peter, with that infallibility with which the Divine Redeemer willed to endow his Church."[20]

It is well known that the Catholic Church claims its leader, the pope, is endowed by God with the charism of infallibility in matters of "faith and morals." What is not so widely appreciated is that the first formal declaration of this doctrine did not come until this moment of crisis when so much was tearing at the fabric of traditional faith and institutional power. Today institutional power is central to the project of Church reform. Absolutist theological claims and institutional universalism have led directly to Church oppression of Jews, to Church condescension toward the laity—especially toward women—and to rejection of freedom of conscience. We shall see in a later chapter how the Church's relationship to these problems is intertwined, in a particular way, with efforts to extend the spiritual and political power of the papacy. The declaration of the infallibility of the pope is therefore a pivotal event. The context within which it occurred tells us everything we need to know about its meaning.

The doctrine of papal infallibility was defined on July 18,

1870,[21] only two days after Napoleon III announced his suicidal mobilization against Prussia and one day before the Franco-Prussian War was formally begun.[22] This Napoleon was heir to the ethos of the French monarchy, not to the republican spirit of the 1789 Revolution. As such, his soldiers had been stationed in Rome as the pope's protectors since 1866. He was the only thing standing between the Roman Catholic Church and the final disaster it had been staving off for centuries. Within weeks of the French declaration of war against Prussia, Napoleon III's army would be routed in a decisive battle at Sedan, a city on the Meuse in northeastern France. Within months, the war would end in the catastrophe of the Paris Commune—and the murder of the archbishop.

In Italy, the Risorgimento, the movement for independence, unification, and constitutional government, was on the rise. The antipapal nationalists, who had succeeded in stripping the pontiff of temporal sovereignty over all the papal territories outside Rome and its environs, were closing in for what the council fathers surely felt was the kill. Popes had exercised political authority over various domains since the fourth century, but the tide of history had turned. In 1791, papal territories in France, centered in Avignon and memorialized in the vintages of Châteauneuf du Pape, had been ripped away by the French Republic. Then, in 1861, Italians under Giuseppe Garibaldi and Victor Emmanuel II had taken the swath of papal land in the midsection of the boot, sweeping up to the second papal city of Bologna.

The opening section of *Pastor Aeternus* makes the thing clear: "And seeing that the gates of hell, with daily increase of hatred, are gathering their strength on every side to upheave the foundation laid by God's own hand, and so, if that might be, to overthrow the Church: we therefore . . . do judge it necessary to propose to the belief and acceptance of all the faithful . . . the doctrine . . . in which is found the strength and solidity of the entire Church."[23]

The imminent "upheaving" of one kind of absolute Church authority therefore required the extraordinary promulgation of another. It was a case of responding, in the scholar Hans Kühner's phrase, to "the political nadir" with "the dogmatic zenith."[24] In reply to questions from reluctant Vatican Council fathers who saw little support in the tradition for the doctrine (some 20 percent opposed the definition of infallibility;[25] once it was voted, 61 bishops walked out in protest), Pope Pius IX declared, "I am the tradition!"[26] Nevertheless, *Pastor Aeternus* refers to the pressing political and social crisis of the moment — "in this very age"[27] — as a justification for its astonishing pronouncement: "Hence we teach and declare that . . . all of whatever rite and dignity, both pastors and faithful, both individually and collectively, are bound, by their duty of hierarchical subordination and true obedience, to submit not only in matters which belong to faith and morals, but also in those that appertain to the discipline and government of the Church throughout the world . . . under one supreme pastor . . . the Roman Pontiff. This is the teaching of the Catholic faith, from which no one can deviate without loss of faith and of salvation."[28]

Obviously, those who were inclined to "deviate" included a swelling population of liberals, republicans, nationalists, and revolutionaries of various kinds. The papacy had made itself the century's bulwark against the new idea. It is "false and absurd or rather mad," Gregory XVI had declared in 1832, "that we must secure and guarantee to each one liberty of conscience;

this is one of the most contagious of errors . . . To this is attached liberty of the press, the most dangerous liberty, an execrable liberty, which can never inspire sufficient horror."[29] Viewed from the twenty-first century, such Church opposition to liberalism, and that opposition's late-twentieth-century renewal during the pontificate of John Paul II, can seem to have been about little more than power, yet the questions underlying this conflict went to the heart of what it is to be human. "The entire liberal world-view appeared to many leading nineteenth-century Catholic theologians," as the sociologist Alan Wolfe sums it up, "to be premised on the notion of the person as a solitary individual lacking connectedness to any sense of meaning or purpose."[30] Indeed, as the twentieth century showed, the legacy of nineteenth-century liberalism would be profoundly ambiguous, but Catholicism, at first, would be attuned far more to what it threatened than to what it promised.

After Vatican I, the operative assumption of the papal absolutists was that there would never be a need for another council, which is why John XXIII's convening of Vatican II was seen at the time as a revolutionary act. In fact, it was deeply traditional. The Church lives through the self-criticism implied in the conciliar process, and not only self-criticism, but self-criticism in response to history. John XXIII's summons was, ipso facto, the call to conscience, and it was an act of hope.

John Henry Newman (1801–1890), the brilliant Englishman who made his name as an Anglican but converted to Catholicism in middle age (1845), was one of those who opposed the move to define papal infallibility as doctrine at Vatican I. When his faction lost out, he found in this long conciliar tradition the reason to remain a Catholic. "Let us have a little faith in her [the

Church] I say. Pius is not the last of the popes. The fourth Council modified the third, the fifth the fourth . . . Let us be patient, let us have faith, and a new Pope, and a reassembled Council, may trim the boat."[31] Newman embodied the Catholic idea that the faith is reasonable, which means that the faith is always subject to reconsideration, and doctrine always subject to development. Hence the conciliar tradition.

When one reads of a Newman, who was able to criticize the Church from within, one feels the sad tug of all those who were lost to Catholicism's endless argument with itself, especially when they were hounded out by a rigid Church establishment. The conciliar tradition assumes theological nuance, and therefore diversity of thought, which suggests that there are places among this people for an Abelard, who sees God's love extended to all people, not just those accepting Jesus, as much as for an Anselm, who sees Jesus saving only those who believe in him; for a hedonistic Renaissance pope friendly to Jews, like Alexander VI, as much as for a puritanical grand-inquisitor pope who establishes the ghetto, like Paul IV. Michelangelo could place a pope in hell in his *Last Judgment,* and as he acted from within the Church, the force of his critique could be felt, as it is today whenever anyone enters the Sistine Chapel; while Voltaire, say, damning the entire apostolic succession, but from outside, remains forever ignored by those who most need to hear his complaint. The great tragedy of the Reformation is that Martin Luther, apparently by a combination of his own impatience and the Church's intolerance, launched his strongest challenges to a decadent Catholicism from outside it.[32] In part for that reason, the Reformation is still waiting to truly happen within the Catholic Church, and it came not enough to the so-called Reformed churches, which, cut adrift, became all too sectarian. Nothing demonstrates that twin set of disappointments better than the post-Reformation fate of the Jews, at the hands of Catholics and Protestants both.

Luther should have been at the great council of the Church that was convened to take up his challenge. At Trent, he might have made his case in a way that prompted something positive from Catholics. Alas, he was long excommunicated by the time that council convened in 1545, and in any case, Luther died the next year, with an anti-Jewish slur on his lips. It is impossible to look back at the Council of Trent without regret that its genuine and partially successful effort at internal reform of Church theology and practice was overshadowed by all that it did to "counter" its enemies outside the Church. Trent responded to the challenge of the reformers by shoring up the battlements — embodied in the rigidity of the Roman catechism, the casuistry of canon law, the violence of the Inquisition, the censorship of the Index, the hatred of nonconformist outsiders, the obsessiveness of rubrical liturgy, the elitism of the clerical estate, and, above all, in the formal establishment of the Roman ghetto — instead of addressing the continent-wide spiritual crisis that Luther, Calvin, and the others had made so dramatic.

Because of the chaos of post-Reformation denominational conflict, the contingencies of revolution, and the philosophical and cultural mutations that accompanied the Enlightenment, the next council, when it finally came in 1869–1870, was unable (to stay with Newman's metaphor) to trim the boat at all. Instead, Vatican I hauled the Church higher into the misanthropic wind, a course that not even John XXIII, given his successors, could change. Still, in this era when the corrosive effects of xenophobic clerical absolutism have been exposed by tragedies as different as the Shoah and the sexual abuse of children, there are reasons to look not only for trimming but for a new tack in fundamental beliefs and practices of the Church. That is why the first conclusion a faithful, if critical, Catholic draws from these tragedies and crimes and all that underlies them is that the time has come to reenvision this religion and the way it relates to the world. The time has come for a gathering of those invested in the future of this Church, which, as is clear by now, means a gathering more broadly defined than any in Church history. Centrally Catholic, it will also include Jews and Protestants, people of other faiths and of no faith, clergy and laity and, emphatically, women.

Thinking symbolically, one might call such a gathering Vatican III, as I and others have, wishing to stress continuity with the reforming council. But after the failure of the Catholic bishops to defend children from abuse—a failure involving a recalcitrant Vatican and, according to some reports, more than half of the American bishops—the time has come to extend the conciliar tradition, not only with token participation of lay and non-Catholic "observers," but with empowered partners from those groups. The bishops cannot resolve this crisis alone, which indicates why, later in this book, I take up the question of democracy in the Church.

Ultimately, it may be nothing less than a "congress" that is required, with all of the democratic implications of that great word. And, equally, it may be that the Vatican is the last place where such a gathering should occur. Perhaps, again for symbolic but grave reasons, the next council of the Catholic Church should take place in Boston, where several egregious cases of child abuse by priests—and protection of the abusers by bishops—were brought to light. Or perhaps, for its great moral reckoning, the world Church should meet in Kraków, near Auschwitz.

Details of the makeup and location of a council, however it is launched, are less significant than the need for a new Church-wide initiative for Catholic reform. Whatever else it might be, Vatican III must be a forum not merely for advancing future change but for recognizing and institutionalizing the massive change, spawned by catastrophes, that is already under way.

3

Reform Proposal 1:
A New Biblical Literacy

ONE REASON to be grateful to the Church of the Counter-Reformation is its resounding rejection not of Martin Luther—I agree with Hans Küng, who proposes a formal lifting, even now, of Rome's excommunication of the reformer,[1] despite his anti-semitism—but of Luther's primal idea that the Christian is to be guided by *sola scriptura,* Scripture alone. In reaction to the abuses of Church authority that drove Luther to his radical stance, he appealed to the ultimate authority of the Bible, as if the texts preceded the community that reads them. But the Catholic position was, and remains, that the community, albeit an inspired one, produced those texts *as* inspired texts, and they are nothing without the readers who take them in. To Luther, Bible readers are individuals who submit to the Word of God as each one understands it, but also as each one bows before it. Luther rejected what appeared to him to be the Church's idolatry of its own hierarchy, but despite his best intentions, he replaced it with a deference to the Word that slips all too easily into an idolatry of its own. Biblical fundamentalism is a manifestation of this. The Catholic-Protestant disagreement goes far deeper than any complaint over indulgences or any political arrangement made with competing princes. Luther "brought the very essence of the Catholic Church into question when (this was the real innovation) he set his personal, subjective, and yet (by his intention) universally binding interpretation of the Scriptures *in principle* above the Church and her tradition."[2]

To Catholics, the understanding of the Scriptures is mediated to the individual by the teaching authority of the Church, which claims primacy over the Word. The Church, after all, began as the communities to which Paul wrote his letters and out of whose oral traditions the Gospels evolved. The Catholic Church understands itself as having canonized (literally, "made a list of") the Word of God, not vice versa. In the twentieth century, when Scripture scholarship blurred the lines between denominations and when the critical-historical method made many of the arguments of the Reformation moot, the Catholic-Protestant difference could seem more a matter of emphasis than substance. But even into the twenty-first century, this difference remains, and is apparent, for example, in the continuing divergence in practice and liturgy, if not theology, that still separates the "Catholic" tradition, with its sacrament-centered cult, from the more "Protestant" tradition, with its Bible-centered cult. But this difference also means that now the community of the Catholic Church, with its claim to authority even over the inspired Word of God, is in a position to confront the problem of foundational texts that have proven themselves to be sources not only of lethal antisemitism but of condescension toward women, suspicion of sexuality, and the misuse of the "apostolic tradition" to justify hierarchical absolutism.

Recognitions in the aftermath of September 11, especially the knowledge that fundamentalist readings of basic texts of many religious traditions can be a danger to the world, put the question of Catholic attitudes toward Scripture squarely at the center of any reform. That is as it should be. After all, we must do more than rearrange the deck chairs on the barque of Peter. By asking, more profoundly, who Peter and his friends (male and female) were, we learn who we can be. By asking who Jesus was to them, we learn who Jesus can yet be to us. Thus the first task facing a new Catholic Church is to foster a broad biblical literacy among the Catholic people. This means recovering a more sophisticated, historically minded understanding of the movement that gave rise to the Church in the first place. And no single issue illuminates that approach more clearly than the primordial opposition between "the Church" and "the Synagogue." Understanding the permanent Jewishness of Jesus, and therefore of Christian faith, is the beginning. And a fuller reckoning with the sources and legacy of anti-Judaism in the New Testament can liberate today's Church from the deadly prison of scriptural fundamentalism, which still has a lock on Catholic attitudes regarding everything from women's ordination to priestly celibacy to the sacred integrity of other religions, beginning with Judaism.

"*Homo sapiens* is the species that invents symbols in which to invest passion and authority," the novelist Joyce Carol Oates once commented, "then forgets that symbols are inventions."[3] The first followers of Jesus were no less human than the rest of us, and this is more or less what they did. After Jesus died, his friends quickly came to understand him in Jewish apocalyptic terms, expecting him to return soon, ushering in the End Time. This is why, for example, Paul counseled his readers to forgo marriage, not because he was antisex but because so little time remained that procreation, that essential investment in an open future, had ceased to have meaning. The assumed imminence of Christ's return informed the first Christians' readiness, even eagerness, to offer their lives as martyrs. The cults of martyrdom and apocalyptic longing go hand in hand.

The first crisis facing the Jesus movement was that its first generation began to die off without seeing the return of the Lord. The Second Coming had proved to be not nearly so imminent as expected. What did it mean, in light of this new experience, to say that Christ's Kingdom had already been established? All at once, this became a pointed question, since whatever else that Kingdom was, the Jews who identified with Jesus assumed it included the liberation of Israel from the oppression of Rome. Around 70 C.E., about forty years after the death of Jesus, Rome's oppression intensified, with the destruction of the Temple in Jerusalem, which compounded the Jewish-Christian crisis of faith. Throughout these years, his followers were telling each other the story of Jesus, in terms taken in part from his biography as they knew it and in part from the Jewish Scripture (the only Scripture there was). These texts provided not only categories (such as "suffering servant") to help them understand who Jesus was, but narrative details with which to elaborate the Jesus story (such as the Seamless Robe and the pierced side, which originate in Psalm 22). This traditional Jewish approach had an unintended negative consequence when the story was told, especially by Gentiles, as a story of Jesus "against" the Jews. The seed of Christian Jew-hatred was planted here, with the old set against the new, with Jews defined as the enemy not only of Jesus but of God, and with Judaism defined as the religion that had outlived God's covenant. Thus the story, particularly the core of it known to us as the Passion narrative—blaming the Roman murder of Jesus on "the Jews," as if Jesus were not a Jew—was, in Oates's term, "invented."

But after the destruction of the Temple, after the followers of Jesus had begun to adjust to the fact that the Lord's return was not imminent, and after the expressly "Jewish" character of the movement was changed by the loss of the cult center of the Temple and by the influx of Gentile converts, the followers "forgot" that the Passion narrative, reflecting *their* conflict with other Jews, was invented. Since Jesus had not returned, they had to do something the first generation had never expected or sought to do, which was to create an apologetic kerygma, or Jesus story, designed to bolster the faith they had in Jesus, both as a way of reassuring one another through a period of crises and as a way of explaining what they believed of Jesus to others, whom they now had to recruit to the movement.

It was at this point that the details of the narrative that had their origin not in the historical life of Jesus but in the Jewish Scriptures were reimagined as "facts." Now the Seamless Robe of Jesus, originating in the psalm, was understood as having actually existed, and the "facts" of its seamlessness and of the centurions' having rolled dice for it were understood as "fulfillments" of the Jewish Scriptures in which those details first appeared. This perception was pressed into service of the apologetic impulse, and all at once the details of the Passion narrative and the pattern of Jewish "foreshadowing" and Christian "fulfillment" became understood as proving the claims that followers of Jesus were making for him. Such proof would have been unthinkable in the first years after the death of Jesus, because the invented character of the story was so well known and because proof was unnecessary in any case, since Jesus was coming back so soon.

Once the story of Jesus took this shape, its rejection by other Jews—who themselves were responding to the trauma of the Temple's destruction—had unprecedented bite. In this post-Temple period, when so much of Jewish culture was destroyed by Rome, only the synagogue-based movement generally associated with the Pharisees had survived to compete with the Jesus movement for the legacy of Israel. When these rabbinic Jews, who were building their identity around the Scriptures, rejected the claims being made by the Christian Jews, the Christians felt threatened because those same Scriptures functioned as their proof. This conflict found its way into the second, third, and fourth iterations of the story Christians were telling each other and newcomers, which is how, in the story, the Pharisees came to be pressed into service as the main antagonists of Jesus, even though, in history, they had been no such thing.

It is helpful to recall the chronology of New Testament composition. Jesus died in the year 30 or so. Within a decade, the story of Jesus, told by his bereaved followers, has begun to take shape, and by around 50 a first written document, referred to by scholars as Q and now lost, compiles the sayings of Jesus. Between about 50 and 60, the letters of Paul are composed, and will form the oldest texts of the New Testament. The earliest Gospel, Mark, dates from 68 or so, and the other three Gospels are written down over the next thirty years.

The incremental nature of Gospel composition, during the years when lament, Scripture study, psalm-singing, remembering, and response to outside pressures marked it, suggests what a human method it was. Thus the Gospels are based partly on what we would call fact—it is a fact that Jesus was executed—

and partly on imagined creations designed to make a theological point, those scriptural details and memories that became altered over time for very human reasons, the most important of which was the Roman war against the Jews. That war, by destroying the Temple and then the entire city of Jerusalem, caused a deep religious crisis in every Jew. And, as wars often do, that one set its victims against each other, Jew against Jew, arguing fiercely over such momentous questions as what it is to be a Jew without the Temple. The record of that intra-Jewish argument is the Gospels—or, as scholars point out, one half of the argument, the Christian half.

So now we can see that, as Christians died, the excruciating death of Jesus took on a meaning, in isolation from his message and life, that it had not had at first. In Luke, Jesus says to the men on the road to Emmaus, "O foolish men . . . Was it not necessary that the Christ should suffer?"[4] Of course, this is not the voice of Jesus but that of his followers, confronted years later with the problem of how to make sense of the suffering they themselves were undergoing. Surely it was suffering at the hands of Rome, as ever. But even more, at the level of meaning they were so desperately clinging to in that traumatic time, it was suffering at the hands of their fellow Jews, who alone could call that meaning into question. So as Christians felt themselves and their movement to be mortally challenged by the refusal of fellow Jews to affirm their messianic understanding of Jesus, it was a small step to lay the actual death of Jesus at the feet not so much of Rome as of these rejecting Jews. Christians accounted for the rejection they were experiencing by making a version of that rejection—"his own people received him not"[5]—central to the experience of Jesus, not just in his Passion but throughout his life.

In this way, by the time the text of John, the last Gospel, is written, around the year 100, "the Jews" are defined as the ontological enemy of Christ. In a contest with antagonists at first identified as "Pharisees," but then as "the Jews," Jesus is remembered as saying to them, "You are from below, I am from above . . . but now you seek to kill me, a man who has told you the truth which I heard from God . . . If God were your Father, you would love me . . . Why do you not understand what I say? It is because you cannot bear to hear my word. You are of your father the devil, and your will is to do your father's desires. He was a murderer from the beginning, and has nothing to do with the truth, because there is no truth in him. When he lies, he speaks according to his own nature, for he is a liar and the father of lies."[6] Jews are cast as the devil. But still—and this remains crucial—it is mainly Jews who are saying so.

If the first followers of Jesus had in their grief invented the first draft of the story in part out of the Jewish Scriptures, subsequent generations invented further drafts from what they had already heard and also from their own experience. The literary genre that came out of this complicated, profoundly human process of invention is not history, nor is it fiction precisely. As scholars remind us, it is, rather, gospel, and in addition to its being profoundly human, it is profoundly Jewish, for the creative interaction between inherited sacred texts and mundane experience is at the heart of what might be called the Midrashic imagination. (Midrash refers to the commentaries and compilations of parable and exegesis with which Jewish scholars respond to Hebrew Scriptures.) The violence of human experience has often been reflected in the works created by that imagination, and the anti-Jewish polemic of, say, John, because of its character as a Jewish invention, stands comparison with the "troubling texts" that imbue the Jewish Scriptures with blood, from those slaughtered firstborn male children in Egypt to the Canaanites driven from Palestine.[7] When the anti-Jewish polemic of John, and the entire New Testament, is read outside the context and in ignorance of the Jewish community that produced it, the words become truly lethal.

The tragedy built into this process is the one Oates identified, namely that people—especially those Gentiles who had no knowledge of Jewish Scriptures and the ways Jews used them —forgot that the Gospel was invented. They forgot not only that it was invented in its details, but that it was invented in its structure. Here we begin to see why *Nostra Aetate* did not go nearly far enough, and what a Third Vatican Council must begin to take up. Yes, the damage done to Jews by the slanderous assertion that they, more than the Romans, put Jesus to death has been incalculable, and as a first order of business that slander has to be repudiated. But the role of "the Jews" as villains in the climactic act of the Passion narrative comes right out of the dramatic structure of the kerygma itself, which puts Jesus in an ontological conflict with his own people of which he would have known nothing. The primal Christian slander against Judaism, rooted in the foundational Christian text, is that Judaism is Christianity's negative other. It is not enough to absolve Jews of the deicide. Is it possible to ask if the entire structure of the Gospel narrative can be criticized as being unworthy of the story it wants to tell?

Similarly with the basic New Testament–Old Testament framework, which gives form to the Christian construct of salvation history. According to that scheme, Israel's prophetic "foreshadowing," which is by definition insubstantial and inferior, is contrasted with the Church's "fulfillment" as the new Israel, or, more polemically, the "true Israel." Although we cannot assume that Jews and Christians will ever approach the Scriptures in the same way, surely Jews have a right to ask: Must the Christian understanding of the very structure of God's Word include the derogatory "replacement theology"[8] that is so often found in the New Testament? When the wrath of an Old Testament God is "replaced" with the love of a New Testament God —and this formulation remains central to Christian preaching —how can Jews not take umbrage at the insult to the Jewish heart such a contrast implies and at the distortion of the fundamental proclamation of Torah, which is God's love?

The technical term for this habit of mind is supersessionism, and a number of Christians, aware of what it can lead to in the post-Holocaust era, have sought to repudiate it. *Nostra Aetate*'s attempt amounted to a first, tentative expression that cried out for elaboration, which, in subsequent commentaries, various officials have tried to supply.[9] Such scholars as the Lutheran Krister Stendahl insist, with similar sensitivity to consequence, that it is wrong to read Saint Paul, as Christians often have, as defining the Church, either in his own life or in history, as a replacement for Israel.[10] "I ask, then, has God rejected his people?" Paul wrote toward the end of his life. "By no means!"[11]

Thus the Church seeks increasingly to affirm, against a dominant Christian tradition, that God's covenant with Israel has never been repudiated. If that is the case, what is the relationship of the "new covenant" of which Jesus speaks at the Last Supper[12] to the preexisting covenant God made at Sinai? Are there two covenants? Separate but equal? Or, if there is one covenant, how do these two divergent experiences of it mesh? Some scholars insist that what Jesus, if he used such language, would actually have been talking about was the "renewed covenant" referred to in Jeremiah,[13] but Jews can still detect in that formulation, offered from outside Judaism, an assumption of replacement. The German Jesuit biblical scholar Norbert Lohfink proposes a single covenant but "a twofold way to salvation,"[14] but the very idea of salvation introduces the question of whether Jews are subsumed in a Christian covenant in the afterlife, which amounts to a postponed religious imperialism. In other words, after nearly two thousand years of reading such texts in one way, we have barely begun to imagine how to read them in another. This project must form the core of Catholic reform.

It is impossible to imagine that the members of a new Vatican Council could return to the early second century and undo what was done in formalizing the New Testament canon, which institutionalized, from the Christian side, the split between Judaism and Christianity. The road not taken then might have led to a religious collaboration between evolving rabbinic Judaism and nascent Christianity, with some kind of mutual notion of the one covenant, binding both currents to the broader stream of the one Israel. But only in a fantasy land do people get to relive such choices and follow such roads to other, wished-for outcomes.

There is no changing the fact that Christianity and Judaism are separate religions, each with distinct integrity that the other must respect. But by recalling that this real outcome, which after all was imagined neither by Jesus nor by Paul, was the result of contingent human choices made in response to accidents of history, the members of Vatican III could understand that no purpose of God's was served by the "parting of the ways" (as scholars refer to the break between Christianity and

Judaism), and that no conclusions about the superiority of one religion or the other should be drawn from it. Furthermore, Vatican III must clearly affirm what has so far been indicated only obliquely, at the level of theology and not official Church teaching—namely, that while Judaism exists without essential reference to Christianity, the reverse is not the case. The God of Jesus Christ, and therefore of the Church, is the God of Israel. The Jews remain the chosen people of God. The Jewish rejection of Jesus as the Son of God is an affirmation of faith that Christians must respect.

The task of Vatican III will be to reorder the Church's relationship to the "troubling texts" that deny all of this. There is no question of simply eliminating them, nor of rewriting them to purge the Epistles and Gospels of what the contemporary ear finds offensive. To some extent, translations can properly soften the edges of the anti-Jewish polemic, substituting, for example, "the leaders" for "the Jews" as the protagonists at the crucifixion, but it would be a mistake to do more to let the Gospels off the hook. Indeed, their offensive character is part of what the Church must learn to admit and to claim. The anti-Jewish texts of the New Testament show that the Church, even in its first generation, was capable of betraying the message of Jesus, establishing once and for all that "the Church as such" can sin. The Church as such stands in need of forgiveness. The Church must therefore preach the anti-Jewish texts of the Gospels— not against the Jews, but against itself. Similarly, the Church must preach antifemale texts, not against women but against itself. Here, as elsewhere, the two problems are related.

In learning to preach in such a way, the Church would be true to its oldest tradition. Christianity has inherited its theological method from Judaism, and that method, perhaps despite itself, is self-critical because biblical faith is self-critical. The prophetic tradition—the prophet Nathan, say, criticizing King David himself—is only the most obvious manifestation of this method, but it is constant. Biblical faith, that is, contains within itself the norms in terms of which biblical faith confesses to having continually fallen short. The Christian problem here, in other words, is a Jewish problem. And the solution is Jewish too. That the first followers of Jesus violated his message by slandering their rivals, even demonizing them, establishes better than anything else that the Church, at its core, is as sinful as any other institution.

Therefore we must have a structure of understanding that enables Christians to read the foundational texts not as divine, as if partaking in the perfection of God, but as invented, to use Oates's word again. That God's Word is "inspired" does not mean it is free of self-contradiction or of tragic consequences. Surely the wonder of inspiration lies in God's use of the inherently flawed medium of the word in the first place. The sin to be repented of, and resisted, is the sin of forgetting that God's Word is human. Much contemporary biblical scholarship assumes this. Vatican III must make the work of such scholarship more widely available in the Church, which means that Christians must be called to a more sophisticated relationship to God's Word. So when they hear the Passion narrative read during Holy Week, they must be helped to hear it not as history but as gospel. To the extent that the texts involve more hate than love, they must be proclaimed as a revelation also of the flawed nature of those who created them. That proclamation of a flawed Gospel, created by flawed believers, leads to what is, after all, good news—that the one whom the Gospel proclaims is the one who will return again to bring this flawed beginning to its completion.

Vatican III, against the long Church tradition of claiming already to be in possession of the fullness of truth, must renew the Christian expectation that there is more to come, exactly because the Kingdom of God is unfinished. Among Jews such an expectation informs messianic hope, but among Christians it takes the form of faith in the Second Coming of the Lord. The measure of this desire is our own present need for it, and the effect of it is self-transcendence. The need for this perspective becomes clear when Jews are murdered, women denigrated, child abuse covered up, laity ignored, all in the name of something holy. The obvious flaws of a Church that has so readily given itself over to hatred reveal the ways in which the "already" is not enough. Any Christian proclamation that says that salvation, redemption, grace, perfection, whatever you call it, has already come is unbelievable on its face. It is also unchristian, because it denies, in the Catholic theologian David Tracy's phrase, "the overwhelmingly 'not-yet' actuality of history itself."[15] A Church that believes it is "as such" incapable of sin—exempt, that is, from the actuality of history—believes it has no need of the return of its Messiah, which may be why the Second Coming of Jesus is rarely the subject of Catholic sermons. But such a Church is also incapable of surpassing itself, which is another way of saying it is dead.

That alone justifies the repudiation of any pretense that the Church, as now constituted, is perfect. "God's revelation in Jesus remains incomplete, unfinished, oriented toward the final manifestation." This is the Vatican II theologian Gregory Baum. "The redemption brought by Jesus to mankind in the present . . . is a token, a pledge, a first installment of the complete redemption promised in the Scriptures . . . But since divine redemption is not finished in Jesus, except by way of anticipation, the Church is not the unique vehicle of grace: room remains in world history for other ways of grace, for many religions, and in particular for the other biblical faith, for Judaism."[16] A renewed Christian longing for the return of the Messiah would rekindle a sharp appreciation for what still binds Jewish and Christian hope.

Martin Buber once remarked to a group of Christians and Jews that both traditions look forward to the coming of the Messiah. Christians believe it will be the Second Coming, while Jews expect it as the first. Buber suggested that Christians and Jews should focus in the meantime on what they have in common, and that when the Messiah finally comes, then "we can ask him whether he's been here before." Robert Nozick, the late Harvard philosopher, loved to tell this anecdote, but with a punch line of his own: "There is only one thing to add to Buber's remarks. I would like to advise the Messiah, when he comes and is asked the question whether he's been here before or not, to reply he doesn't remember."[17]

The future beckons like the horizon, but the past imposes its harsh judgment, and, likewise, one paramount duty: the Church must be responsible for the real-world consequences of its most troubling texts. Never again must worshipers leave a church on Good Friday looking for Jews to attack. Never again must women be made to feel unequal, never again the crimes of priests covered up in the name of Peter's primacy. Therefore the act of reading such texts must now involve the act of arguing against them. The inherently supersessionist terminology of "Old" and "New" Testaments must be replaced.[18] Likewise "Law" and "Gospel." Instead of an inherently contemptuous tension between Jewish "prophecy" and Christian "fulfillment," Vatican III must invite a new sensitivity to what Stendahl calls the "tender typology," according to which Christians and Jews both could recognize the shape of God's way of acting in history and through time. There must be a resonance between Jewish and Christian narratives (Passover and Easter) that does not involve the superiority of one over the other.

Specifically, in moving beyond *Nostra Aetate*, the distortions that appear in the New Testament, whether of the behavior of "the Jews" or of the theology of Torah, would be flagged as such — and confessed as such. Vatican III must help Christians learn to read anti-Jewish texts as if they were themselves Jews (and antifemale texts as if they were all women, and, for that matter, as I heard a Jewish scholar say, anti-Canaanite texts as if they were Canaanites).[19] The texts themselves call the Church to this, because finally they do enshrine the authentic presence of Jesus Christ — not the "historical" Jesus exactly, but the real and living Jesus as confessed by those who knew him, confessed above all as the embodiment of love. Remembered as one who called every act of hatred into question, therefore including hatred of "the Jews," Jesus is nevertheless remembered also as one who never assumed that his adherents would follow his example perfectly. The Church's memory of Jesus Christ "releases the theological knowledge that there is no innocent tradition," as David Tracy puts it, "no innocent classic, no innocent reading."[20] Indeed, the figure of Jesus presented by the Gospels, the one who forgives not once, not seven times, but seventy times seven, is clear on the point that all humans, and therefore all human texts, stand equally in need of forgiveness.

Jesus is never more "Jewish" than here, never more faithful to the one covenant with the One God. Vatican III could call as a witness Rabbi David Hartman. "The confirmation of human beings in their human limitation is the soul of the covenantal message," Hartman says. "The covenant is not God's desire for humanity to escape from history, but God's gracious love saying that humanity in its finite temporal condition is fully accepted by the eternal God . . . Can we love God in an imperfect way and in an imperfect world? . . . History is not the revelation of eternal truth, but God's ability to love us in our imperfection."[21]

The fear, envy, insecurity, despair, grief, male supremacy, and hatred that corrupted the authors of the New Testament do not destroy the Church. The marvel is, they establish it.

4

Reform Proposal 2:
The Church and Power

THERE ARE FEW things we can say with more cer-
tainty about Jesus than that he defined his mission in
opposition not to Judaism but to the imperium of
Rome. Rome's contempt for the peoples it had sub-
jugated, Rome's ruthless violence, Rome's worship of itself,
Rome's substitution of Caesar for God—Jesus said no to it all.
Whether his message is understood to have been messianic,
apocalyptic, magical, cynical, revolutionary, or "merely" spiritual, it is clear that he invited his followers to join him in rejecting Rome. The ambiguous nature of the early Church's relationship to Rome—one reason the Gospels highlighted Jews
instead of Romans as enemies of Jesus was to avoid trouble with
the empire, perhaps especially after Nero's brutal scapegoating
of Christians in the decade of the sixties—takes nothing away
from the primal Christian critique of power. Once Paul turned
the tragic fate of Jesus against those who had caused it—
turned the cross, that is, against the legion's standard—the
story of Jesus swept the world over which Caesar held sway because it spoke intimately to those whose throats were under
Rome's heel. The Gospel took root in the soul of powerlessness,

which is why, to this day, it beckons the dispossessed in ways it does no other group.

But the Church has never truly come to terms with the contradiction it embraced when the Roman imperium and Roman Catholicism became the same thing. That tremendous reversal occurred around 312 when the emperor Constantine accepted the Christian faith and then used it as the unifying ideology underwriting the extension of his imperial sway from the north of Europe to North Africa. He ordered the abolition of crucifixion as a means of capital punishment, thinking of Jesus, but he also taught his soldiers to shape the cross by tying their knives to their spears. And his mother, Saint Helena, just then "discovering" the True Cross—led to it, in the myth, by a treasonous Jew —helped to put that symbol where Caesar's eagle had been. The transformation of the cross was complete: not a sign of real suffering any longer, nor even, with Paul, of spiritualized victory, but a sign of power in the world. "The power of the cross of Christ," Athanasius of Alexandria declared, "has filled the world."[1]

The point is not to wish sentimentally that the Christian religion, in order to maintain its purity, had remained the marginal cult of a despised minority, with an ad hoc organization; more charismatic than catholic; possessing nothing; being more acted upon than a spur to action; and innocent, not in the sense of sinless but in the sense of untested, untouched. The glory of the Church includes what its institutionalization has enabled: a transcending of time and culture, a triumph over history that stands alone. Every Catholic is proud to be part of a two-thousand-year-old tradition that still lives. But such longevity presumes a weighty bureaucracy. It presumes possession, even wealth. It presumes the great contests of will between rulers and popes, princes and bishops, masters and monks. It presumes the wily strategies that survival required. It presumes the yoking of intellect to piety, and the adaptation of faith to Plato's separation of form and matter, to Aristotle's rational quest for universal order, and ultimately to Kierkegaard's leap into the arbitrary. It even presumes the admission of politics to pulpits, and perhaps the conscription of cloisters into service as bastions. The ruins of Europe, the museums of Europe, the cathedrals and castles and Gothic-towered universities of Europe, are the stone record of this story, and though there is cold shame in it, there is carved beauty too. The history of the Church, not above the world but in it, only continues what we just saw revealed by the Church's troubling foundational texts—that the Church is of the human condition, not against it.

But a Vatican III could ask the question of whether the Church, responding to an emperor's self-interest, assumed too much the emperor's ethos. Assumed it so much, in fact, that the emperor's ethos—more, say, than Augustine's adaptation of Plato, Aquinas's of Aristotle, Francis's of Jesus—is what most indelibly stamps the soul of Catholicism. Why is that? Pope John Paul II took a first stab at asking this troubling question when, at his millennial Mass of repentance in March 2000, he acknowledged that "Christians have often denied the Gospel, yielding to a mentality of power."[2] That confession, strong as it is, points beyond itself to what has not been confessed yet. Obviously, more than the behavior of "Christians" is at issue here, and, for that matter, more than a "mentality" is too. A Vatican III could push further into this problem, asking if it is at last possible to reverse Constantine and reclaim the cross for Jesus Christ and for those who are left out of every imperial victory, or rather, defeated by it.

Regardless of whether such a council would take up the question, history does. That is the meaning, finally, of the "interruption" of history experienced during the Holocaust. In light of that event as the outcome of the long narrative begun at Milvian Bridge, where Constantine had a "vision" of the cross, heretofore unquestioned Christian assumptions suddenly seem tragically problematic — and not only in relation to Jews. The need for Catholic reform is evident wherever we see the sin of the Church, and the recent priest abuse scandal, tied to questions of sexuality and gender, become a scandal tied expressly to power when bishops put the clerical state ahead of children. This shows that antisemitism and sexism are connected — and it is significant that they infected the marrow of the Church at the same time, in the same circumstance. When children become sexually vulnerable to disturbed men, we are an inch away from the question of what those men, and also their protectors, make of women. Real reform after the child abuse scandal begins, that is, when we ask, What are the heretofore unquestioned Catholic assumptions about women?

"Christian biblical theology must recognize," the Catholic feminist theologian Elisabeth Schüssler Fiorenza has written, "that its articulation of anti-Judaism in the New Testament goes hand in hand with its gradual adaptation to Greco-Roman patriarchal society. Christian as well as Jewish theology must cease to proclaim a God made in the image and likeness of Man. It can do so only when it mourns the 'loss' of women's contributions in the past and present and rejects our theological 'dehumanization.' Moreover, white Christian and Jewish theology must promote the full humanity of all non-Western peoples and at the same time struggle against racism wherever it is at work. In short the memory of the Holocaust must 'interrupt' all forms of Western patriarchal theology if the legacies of the dead are not to be in vain."[3]

This problem of the Church's attitude toward women goes to the heart of the present crisis of priests' sexuality. That the scandal has surfaced a deep skepticism among Catholics about priestly celibacy is not to simplistically place the blame there for problems unique to pedophiles. But clearly the makeup of the sexual imagination of the Church itself is now an open question. The patriarchal misogyny of the clerical culture is broadly discredited, perhaps for the first time. And nothing challenges this hypermale tradition more directly than the witness of women.

Altering the Church's "mentality of power" presumes a fundamental shift in its attitude toward the "other," which in this defensively and exclusively male culture is quintessentially the woman. A power structure that denigrates women is the most basic manifestation of the binary opposition that has simultaneously, if far more violently, oppressed Jews. While it may seem unrelated to Jewish-Christian conflict, a feminist critique of theology and practice is central to it, because feminism seeks not a mere substitution of female privilege for male privilege, but a dismantling of the entire structure of binary opposition in favor of authentic mutuality. Specifically, a feminist reading of the New Testament, as we have in a scholar like Elisabeth Schüssler Fiorenza, reveals, for example, that the women who followed Jesus, unlike the men, "understood that his ministry was not rule and kingly glory but *diakonia*, 'service' (Mark 15:41). Thus the women emerge as the true Christian ministers and witnesses."[4] The mentality of power is the issue, and as the Gospels display a treasonous anti-Judaism, they also reveal, in the anonymity of these very women, assumptions of male dominance that must equally be rejected.

The readiness with which the Church put itself at the service of the self-preserving and patriarchal imperium has long been an untied knot of the Catholic conscience, from Constantine in his wars against his rivals, to the brown robes at the side of Spanish conquistadors, to the priests who blessed King Leopold's African loot, to the 1933 display of Catholic obeisance before Adolf Hitler, embodied in the Reichskonkordat, the Vatican's sanctioning treaty with Hitler. The Church's failure to oppose the rise of Nazism remains the most dramatic instance of what requires reform. That failure, enabled by Eugenio Pacelli, who negotiated that treaty, and sealed by Pacelli as the "silent" Pius XII, involved a choice *for* papal power and *against* not only Jews but the German Catholic Church. And papal power was the key.

The long history that comes after Constantine demonstrates that the "modern" pursuit of such power drives relentlessly along the unbroken shaft of apostolic succession, from Leo I (440–461), with his initiating universal claims; to Gregory VII (1073–1085), who bested the emperor at Canossa and, against the Greeks, claimed sovereignty over the whole Church; to Urban II (1088–1099), who launched the First Crusade (and Europe's first pogrom) with the cry "God wills it!"; to Innocent III (1198–1216), who extended the claim of papal sovereignty to the whole world (and imposed the yellow star on Jews); to Boniface VIII (1294–1303), who decreed that every king, indeed every creature, is a vassal of the pope; to Paul IV (1555–1559), who, asserting authority over the human mind, established the Index of Forbidden Books (and the Roman ghetto); to Pius IX (1846–1878), who claimed papal primacy over the council, and papal infallibility over "faith and morals" (while kidnapping a Jewish child); to Pius XII (1939–1958), who put papal power above meeting the moral challenge of his century; to John Paul II (1978–), who, against the great exception John XXIII, and despite his own evident good will, devotes himself to the continuation of this tradition.

It is in the context of this tradition that we must see the Vatican's recent refusal to hold bishops fully accountable for their protection of pedophile priests. These priests, too, are beneficiaries of a top-down hierarchy organized to protect itself no matter what—no matter the cost to Jews, certainly, and no matter the cost to children. "Power corrupts," Lord Acton is well known for saying, "and absolute power corrupts absolutely." What is less well known, as Garry Wills points out, is that the British aristocrat was a Catholic opposed, in 1870, to the dogma of papal infallibility, and the power he was warning of was the pope's.[5]

Let us suppose that the ecumenically composed membership of Vatican III meets in St. Peter's Basilica, as the fathers of Vatican I and Vatican II did. On the subject of power, the place itself can be a prod to action. In my dictionary, "basilica" is defined as "a privileged Catholic church," but the word comes from *basileus,* for "king," and among Romans it referred to Caesar's palace— literally to Constantine's palace, the *Konstantin-basilika.* The emperor, that is, was the originator of this architecture as the dominant church form. The soaring central nave of St. Peter's, · with the semicircular apse at the far end, is modeled after the palaces Constantine built for himself. The design enhances the stature of the figure who occupies the throne in the distant apse, and in St. Peter's that throne, behind and above the altar, belongs not to God but to the popes. Lining both side aisles of the mammoth hall are the massive imperial tombs in which Roman popes are buried, sarcophagi worthy of the potentates so many of them aspired to be. In the towering cupola above the transept is the mythic inscription *Tu es Petrus . . .*, as if the peasant Jesus ordained all this.

Whatever historical contingencies led to the cult of papal omnipotence—from the empire of antiquity to the investiture disputes with medieval kings, from the Renaissance glorification of genius to the assaults of reformation and revolution—can a member of Vatican III cast his or her eyes around this shrine to the imperium and ask if its time has finally gone? When John XXIII stepped down from his throne to sit as an equal among a delegation of Jewish visitors, was he hinting at the necessary shift? And when his council transformed the Catholic liturgy by eliminating the secret language of the court in favor of the language spoken by all, and by replacing the high altar with a simple table, which required the priest to come down as Pope John himself had done, was the shift being further prepared for? "Power to the people," we learned to say in our youth, and because of a revolution begun at the Church's top, we Catholics had a first taste of the "popular" religion that subsequent popes would try to turn back. But how do you turn back a tide? "It is quite clear," David Tracy told the *New York Times* in 1986, "that Catholicism is going through the greatest change since its passage from a Jewish sect to a Greco-Roman religion. The ways of being a Catholic will necessarily multiply and the Church will be more diverse; pluralism in religious expression will increase, not decrease."[6] Vatican II defined the Church as the People of God, and Vatican III must make the definition real by reordering the Church according to its new self-understanding.

The papacy must be restored as an office of *diakonia,* service, to be exercised in partnership with other Christians (not just Catholics, not just bishops and priests, and not just men). Extending Elisabeth Schüssler Fiorenza's insight into the link between patriarchy and anti-Judaism, it is notable that the pope who instituted the *Sicut Judaeis* tradition of defending Jews and forbidding their forced conversion, Gregory I (590–604), was also the pope who defined his function as being not *Papa,* an ultimate patriarch, but, as he put it, "servant of the servants of God."[7] As Hans Küng points out, Gregory was the author of perhaps the most influential work written by a pope, *Pastoral Rule,* which located the soul of ministry in personal example and in service—real acts of meeting human needs—not in the concentration of control and not in the preempting of local leadership. The phrase "pastoral rule" can be taken as a rebuttal of "holy rule," which is the meaning of "hierarchy."[8] That this pope is called "the Great," one of only two so honored, suggests that the witness of such a life, as with John XXIII, weighs more in the balance than the witness of popes who take their greatness for granted. That Gregory's rejection of patriarchal triumphalism was accompanied by a sense of obligation to the well-being of Jews is no coincidence. As the history of antisemitism suggests, as long as the Church defines itself triumphalistically, Jews remain a living contradiction to all such claims, and the offense taken by Christians at their "prophetic critique refused"[9] is squared. It is then that Christians become most dangerous to Jews.

St. Peter's Basilica enshrines the problematic history of Church power, but it also enshrines the "dangerous memory" of Jesus Christ, which remains the "countermemory to all tales of triumph," Tracy says. "Christianity is always a memory that turns as fiercely against itself as against other pretensions to triumph . . . To become historically minded is to seize that memory for the present and to recall the past in that memory's subversive light."[10] Among Catholics, the main custodian of the antitriumphal impulse has been the tradition of Church councils that have steadily, if imperfectly, checked the temptation to papal imperium. Therefore, in the name of the authentic Catholic tradition, and to counter the universalist absolutism that underwrites all "pretensions to triumph," the conciliar principle—the bishop of Rome exercising authority accountably, within the college of bishops—must be reestablished, and now extended to include the laity. Due regard for the regional autonomies of bishops, the cultural distinctions of local churches, and the idea that all Christians share the priestly office must be retrieved. It is in this context that the Catholic Church can at last honor the various regional differences that gave rise to most Protestant and Orthodox denominations. The primacy-enforcing ideas of Roman supremacy and papal infallibility, based as both are on a shallow urge toward certitude, reflect the universalizing pseudoscience of the Enlightenment more than the Gospel.

The members of Vatican III owe it to themselves "to become historically minded," in Tracy's phrase, including becoming more fully acquainted with the bizarre political and personal circumstances of Vatican I that prompted its fathers to issue *Pastor Aeternus.* Knowing of the nationalist siege that was closing in on them, we can honor their good intentions, sympathize with their fears, and salute their loyalty to the pope while forthrightly acknowledging that the definition of papal infallibility was a mistake. Twentieth-century Church history, with the Holocaust as its epiphany, establishes it as such, down to and including the inability of Pope John Paul II to say of Pius XII,

"What my predecessor did, and what he failed to do, in the crucible of 'faith and morals' was wrong."[11] The defining of the doctrine of papal infallibility amounts to the low point in the long story of patriarchy, a legitimation of Church exceptionalism, a reversal of the meaning that Jesus gave to ministry, and, finally, an abuse of power. Instead of trying to slide past the embarrassment of the blunder, or hoping that the doctrine will wither into disuse over time, Vatican III—since the point is to acknowledge fallibility—should repeal it.

5

Reform Proposal 3:
A New Christology

G OD IS GREATER than religion . . . ," Rabbi Abraham Joshua Heschel wrote. "Faith is greater than dogma."[1] If the human species is by nature inclined to forget that its creation myths are just that — created myths — it is also true that its most absolutely asserted dicta are the products of relative intellectual constructs that are rarely recognized as such. After September 11, the world knows with urgent freshness that theologies of all kinds are tied to real-world political consequences. That is obviously true of a theology that declares "jihad," but it is also true of a theology that spawned "crusade." President Bush's use of that word to define the American War on Terrorism, even if inadvertent, was a signal of the deep, often unconscious connection between belief and politics. Indeed, the inadvertence makes the point. Every religion must now make that connection the subject of a grave examination of conscience.

For that reason Vatican III must initiate a Church-wide reimagination of sacrosanct theologies, or rather, sponsor the Church-wide dissemination of the inventive work that theologians have already been doing. Such a project is necessary because, however much intended as timeless acts of devotion, sacrosanct theologies have underwritten violence, intolerance, sexism, sexual neurosis, and antisemitism. Indeed, a theological recovery from all that leads to a hatred of Jews can show what is needed overall. An example of this theological reconsideration of fundamental texts and dogmas, in light of the Church's historic negation of Judaism, is the work of Rosemary Radford Ruether, whose classic formulation of the problem—Christology, or the basic theology of Christ, as "the other side of anti-Judaism"[2]—remains unaddressed by the Church. The Church has yet to face, in David Tracy's phrase, "the revolting underside of Christology in the history of Christian antisemitism."[3]

A brief look at the era of the Crusades, when politics and theology came together in tragic ways, can illuminate the source of this problem as it still exists and how we might leave it behind. The launching of the First Crusade, in 1096, is widely regarded as the time Europe began to wake from the slumber of its Dark Age. The Crusades both reflected and advanced a vigorous new social movement. Intercultural exchange, and with it the return of rationalism, reflected in theology's new preoccupation with "proving" the existence of God, led to a renaissance in the West. But the Dark Age itself was, in part at least, an unintended consequence of powerful but ambiguous developments occurring in Christian theology, an intellectual equivalent of the Church's political accommodation of the imperium in the aftermath of Constantine's conversion. The theological formulations that jelled between the Council of Nicaea (325) and the Council of Constantinople (381) had reflected an accommodation with Greek thought, and so had the work of the great Augustine (354–430). In this period, the metaphors that early Christians used to describe their experience of and faith in

Jesus of Nazareth were reinvented in the categories of Hellenistic metaphysics. Obviously, the movement from religious expression, which began essentially as poetry and which prizes ambiguity and allusiveness, to religious philosophy, which values precision above implication, represents a decisive shift.

When the Church fathers found the mysteries of revelation to be illuminated by their understanding of Plato's dichotomy between form and matter—between the world, that is, of ideal perfection and the inherently flawed material world of everyday experience—a new idea of the cosmos braced the Christian vision. Less a construct of Plato than of his syncretist interpreters of late antiquity, especially Plotinus (c. 205–270), Neo-Platonism posited a dualism that would become Christianized as between grace and sin. This was one culture's form of the perennial human inclination toward binary thinking, as evidenced among Gnostics of various kinds in the ancient world. The Neo-Platonic divide between soul and body would have its later equivalents in the post-Descartes alienation between the self and the world, and even in the postmodern deconstruction of the bond between the self and the self's expression.

Now God was understood to be the True, the One, the Holy; the material world—enigmatic, chaotic, profane—could only be ontologically unrelated to such a God. Creation was merely the Creator's shadow. For a people with roots in the biblical view of reality, this was a massive mutation, for the God of Israel, while very much a transcendent God, was the Lord of human history who had chosen to be intimately involved in that history. Among Christians, a new idea of the person took hold too, one equally foreign to the biblical idea, with a split between the body and the soul, which in nature could not be reconciled. This split posed large problems for theologians who sought to define exactly how Jesus could be both God and man, and disagreements over the formulas constructed to answer the question—"begotten, not made," "hypostatic union," "*filioque*"—became violent, leading to the first great condemnations of heresy.

But perhaps the most damaging consequence of this new dualism was the devaluation of the physical world that seemed logically to flow from a Neo-Platonic suspicion of "matter." This led not only, say, to the distrust of sexual pleasure (original sin defined as the sex act)—which was powerfully symbolized by the new idea that priests should be celibate—but also to the reduction of women to their sexuality. That, ipso facto, rendered women ritually impure, disqualifying them more than ever from true equality. And make no mistake: this primitive, thoroughly unchristian notion of female ritual impurity has far more to do with the prohibition of women's ordination than with the gender makeup of the apostles, no matter what the Vatican says.

The problem went beyond sex and gender, however, for the undergirding idea was that human beings, mired in the material world, were inherently unable to arrive at a state of happiness—in religious language, salvation—that was natural to the realm of the ideal. The body, that is, condemned the soul to live in permanent exile from the realm for which it was made. It is only when such Hellenistic categories shape Christian theology that the idea of the immortality of the soul becomes the content of religious hope—a notion that has nothing in common with biblical hope, which is based on personal wholeness, not dichotomy; on God's promise, not the soul's indestructibility. But in the scheme of Christian Neo-Platonism, even the soul's intrinsic immortality was no hope, because its pollution by the body left it doomed.

The gulf between body and soul was itself a pale shadow of the infinitely larger gulf between God and the human person. One effect of this thoroughgoing Hellenization of the meaning of Jesus, whatever positive results it had as an intellectual construct, was the obliteration of the Jewish aspect of that meaning. With the Christian adoption of Greek intellectual categories, the parting of the ways between Church and Synagogue became turnpikes set in concrete. From now on, most ominously, since there was nothing intrinsically Jewish about Jesus, there would be nothing to prevent Christians from defining themselves in opposition to Jews.

Despite the intellectual monuments created by Church fathers from Tertullian to Augustine, a collapse of intellectual pursuit and scientific inquiry was an ultimate consequence of the Christian adoption of a dualistic worldview, since there was no reason to take the experience of the senses seriously. On the contrary, the senses became the enemy, and where once the sexual body was celebrated as the image of God — "So God created man in his own image, in the image of God he created him; male and female he created them"[4] — the sexual body now became an "occasion of sin" to be subdued. Among Christians, the Greek idea of soul became entirely removed from the biblical idea of spirit, which, since it literally means "breath," is intrinsically physical. Now the body, even with its breath, was defined as the source of all evil. Priests became celibate. Christian piety became penitential — the self-flagellation of body hatred became the highest form of devotion — and even the work of the mind, like reading and study, because dependent on the senses, became defined as worldly distraction. A culture based on such assumptions was bound to shrivel, and the culture of Western Europe did just that.

And so too with Christology. The memory of Jesus was

pressed into service as the antidote to the despair that flowed from such dualism. If the gulf between heaven and earth, between soul and body, was infinite, then the infinite Son of God alone could bridge it. The coming of Jesus was now defined as God's effort to repair the fallen creation, and consistent with the new attachment to flagellation, the flagellation of Jesus — the punishment of his body — took on an importance it had not had for early Christians. The Son of God could bridge the gulf between Creator and creation, between soul and body, only by the destruction of his body. The Passion and death became the heart of the meaning of Jesus' life. The cross became the essential icon of faith, and the fact that these systems of belief affected the realm of politics is revealed by the coming of the war of the cross, the Crusades. It can be no surprise that this combination of theology and politics inevitably escalated the Church's war against the Jews, with those First Crusaders murdering thousands of Jews in cities along the Rhine in the spring of 1096.

Ironically, the highest form of this philosophically dualistic Christology came with the publication, in 1098, of what scholars consider the most influential theological treatise ever written, *Cur Deus Homo.* This was an explanation by Saint Anselm (1033–1109) of "why God became human." I say ironically because it is also true that Anselm's embrace of the rational method, and his trust in the essentially physical process of thought, marked a turn away from anti-intellectualism and anti-corporeality. Indeed, Europe's recovery from the legacy of a rigid Neo-Platonism would be tied largely to what Anselm helped initiate, the reacquaintance with Aristotle, his celebration of the unity of being as opposed to its dichotomy. In contrast to Neo-Platonic "idealism," Aristotle's "realism" defines the sensed world as real and not just as the insubstantial and inferior shadow of a higher realm. Such a real world is worthy of careful scrutiny, and only such a system of thought can support scientific inquiry. The return of Aristotle meant the return of *scientia,* which was the precondition for the thriving of the universities. Anselm, with his own trust in the rational method, marks the beginning of Europe's Aristotelian recovery.

Anselm was a Lombardy-born monk who went on to become Archbishop of Canterbury, but as a scholar he was among the first outside Iberia to benefit from that peninsula's great collaboration of Muslim and Jewish translators, which helped restore Aristotle to Europe. But Anselm's Christology reflected Neo-Platonic dualism more than Aristotelian unity of being, and that dualism survives vigorously in the Church, as its attitudes toward Jesus, and toward sexuality, reveal.

Here is how the Catholic theologian Elizabeth Johnson summarizes Anselm's significance:

> In the eleventh century the biblical and patristic pluralism so characteristic of interpretations of Jesus and salvation began to recede in the West due to Anselm's brilliant restructuring of the satisfaction metaphor into a full-fledged ontologically based theory. To wit: God became a human being and died to pay back what was due to the honor of God offended by sin. I sometimes think that Anselm should be considered the most successful theologian of all time. Imagine having almost a one-thousand-year run for your theological construct! It was never declared a dogma but might just as well have been, so dominant has been its influence in theology, preaching, devotion, and the penitential system of the Church, up to our own day.[5]

Anselm's idea is that the work of Jesus was "salvation" — saving those who believed in him from the impossible abyss that separated God from humanity, bridging it with his own body. But just as previous generations had forgotten the invented character of their sacred narratives, the heirs of the world shaped by Christian Platonism assumed that the gulf across which Jesus had to lay his body was created by God in reaction to the Fall, and not by the ancient interpreters of Plato. Religiously, they would have said it was the sin of Adam that had made an enemy of God, but actually their religious language was conditioned by a philosophical presumption that was enshrined by now in piety, if not dogma, that divided heaven from earth. Just because an intellectual schema dubbed God as hostile and unavailable did not mean God was any such thing. But who was to say that?

Because Anselm was operating out of the belief system of feudal politics, he took God to be an overlord whose insulted sense of justice required an act of "satisfaction" equal to the initial affront God had suffered, the original sin. Since the one affronted was infinite, Anselm reasoned, the one offering satisfaction had to be infinite, which is why Jesus had to be divine. And since the affront was an abuse of human freedom, it could be overturned only by an act of human freedom, which is why Jesus had, equally, to be human. Death is the wages of sin, and since Jesus was without sin, he in no way deserved to die. Therefore only by his free choice could he die, but that free choice was the only thing that would satisfy the affronted God. So Jesus *had* to die, and his death would save the world. Thus ran the links of Anselm's chain of reason.

By choosing his fate on the cross, Jesus was, as the theologian Jaroslav Pelikan helps us understand, getting God to change

God's mind about creation, getting the punitive God of the Old Testament, that is, to stop being the enemy of all that God had made. Jesus, the bridge between the otherwise irreconcilable human and divine, was "saving" creation by getting God to love it again. The Gospel replaced the Law. Grace replaced sin. The new Adam replaced the old. This dualistic progression perfectly matched the supersessionist assumption that by now was the central pillar of the Church. And not incidentally, the locus of this transformation was a particular place. The execution precinct outside Jerusalem, where the cross was planted, was itself the site of the defeat of doom, but doom defined as within the scope of Judaism. When Pope John Paul II called Auschwitz the "Golgotha of the modern world"[6] in 1979, he was thinking of Anselm's Golgotha. The pope spoke only with good intentions, but there was a problem, for at Anselm's Golgotha God had intruded in time, turning time against the Jews. At Golgotha their time was up. And why should Jews not have been offended to hear Auschwitz so referred to?

The first result of Anselm's theology of salvation (soteriology) was to solder the faith to the cross, and to make the death of Jesus more important than anything he had said, despite his clear statement that "the words that I have spoken to you are spirit and life."[7] His death counted for more than his having been born, having lived as a Jew, having preached a gospel of love in the context of Israel's covenant with a loving God, having opposed the imperium of Rome, even having been brought to the new life of Resurrection. The death obsession of the flagellants was deemed holy, and the blood lust of the Crusaders was sanctified. God, too, had blood lust. Christ's agony on the cross would now become the black flower of the Western imagination—on armor, in Passion plays, in paintings, in altar carvings, in rituals like the Stations of the Cross, and ultimately in a cross erected by Polish Catholics at Auschwitz.

The second result of atonement soteriology was more damaging, for Jews and for everyone else who declined to put Jesus at the center of hope. Jesus Christ was defined as the one solution to a cosmic problem. Understood as reordering creation, as redeeming an otherwise doomed world, he was seen as the only way to God. Because of this cosmic and ontological accomplishment of Jesus Christ, understood as bringing about an "objective" adjustment in creation and a change in the Godhead, Christianity views itself, in the words of the twentieth-century Catholic theologian Karl Rahner, as "the absolute and hence the only religion for all men."[8] When the Vatican issued its apology in 2000 for using "methods not in keeping with the Gospel in the solemn duty of defending the truth,"[9] it seemed content to acknowledge its flawed "methods" without confronting the problem of the "truth" that was being defended, which was this absolute claim for the Catholic religion. In fact, the flawed "methods" (the Crusades, the Inquisition) revealed the flawed "truth."

Karl Rahner saw this. He was a German Jesuit whose first professorial post, at Innsbruck, was eliminated when the Nazis closed the Catholic universities in 1936. He spent the war years teaching religious education in Vienna,[10] and after the war his openly expressed appreciation of the need for a reconsideration of Catholic dogma led to his being silenced by the Vatican. No theologian's rehabilitation by Pope John's Vatican II was more dramatic. Rahner's great effort, toward the end of his life, was to reconcile the traditional claim for Jesus as the universal source of all salvation with its plainly negative effects. "The West is no longer shut up in itself," Rahner wrote; "it can no longer regard itself simply as the center of the history of this world and as the center of culture, with a religion which . . . could appear as the obvious and indeed sole way of honoring God." And he goes on to observe, in the line referred to earlier, "Today everybody is the next-door neighbor and spiritual neighbor of everyone else in the world . . . which puts the absolute claim of our own Christian faith into question."[11]

Puts into question, that is, the idea that only the freely chosen death of Jesus appeased the condemning wrath of God. If Anselm is right, in other words, then there is no salvation apart from the Church (as the popes would say) or, at the very least, apart from an "anonymous" (as the more liberal-minded Rahner dubbed it) relationship to Jesus — a relationship, say, that a Torah-revering Jew might have, even without knowing it. The "absolute religion" must regard all other religions as inferior, if not venal. "Anonymous Christians," by virtue of their good conscience whatever its religious basis, are conscripted into the Church without knowing it, whether they want to be or not.[12]

Here is where the work of a Vatican III would begin, for it is impossible to reconcile this Christology, these cosmic claims for the accomplishment of Jesus Christ as the one source of salvation, with authentic respect for Judaism and every other "spiritual neighbor." And if anything has changed in the early twenty-first century, it has been the new awareness of the pluralistic religious "neighborhood" in which all people live now. Because it trumps not only the faith of other believers but the freedom of God to move in creation, the Church's fixation on the death of Jesus as the universal salvific act must end, and the place of the cross must be reimagined in Christian faith.

As long as an understanding of God as having been changed from wrathful to loving by the freely chosen death of Jesus remains central to Church attitudes, any effort at interreligious amity will be false, for below the universalist claim of this "absolute religion" abides the flinty substratum of the old contempt. This is why Rahner could observe that "the pluralism of religions . . . must therefore be the greatest scandal and the greatest vexation for Christianity."[13]

And so, among key Catholic prelates, it is. In October 1999 there convened a synod of European bishops. A working document (*instrumentum laboris*) prepared by Vatican officials included this statement:

> Pluralism has taken the place of Marxism in cultural dominance, a pluralism which is undifferentiated and tending toward skepticism and nihilism . . . In the context of the present increasing pluralism in Europe, the synod also intends to proclaim that Christ is the one and only savior of all humanity and, consequently, to assert the absolute uniqueness of Christianity in relation to other religions . . . Jesus is the one and only mediator of salvation for all of humanity. Only in him do humanity, history and the cosmos find their definitively positive meaning and receive their full realization. He is not only the mediator of salvation, but salvation's source.[14]

The Vatican of John Paul II was so intent on defining religious pluralism as the great modern evil that, in 1997, it excommunicated a Sri Lankan theologian, Tissa Balasuriya, an "Asian Rahner" whom the Church he had served for half a century denigrated as a "relativist." Balasuriya's offense? Daring to imply that Hinduism and Buddhism might be authentic ways to God. Not even Hans Küng, who directly challenged papal infallibility, had been excommunicated (nor, for that matter, had Hitler).[15]

This campaign against "the rapid spread of the relativistic and pluralistic mentality" was carried forward more vigorously in September 2000 when the Vatican issued "*Dominus Iesus:* On the Unicity and Salvific Universality of Jesus Christ and the Church," a surprising reiteration of the Roman Catholic triumphalism most thought had been buried at Vatican II.[16]

I will have more to say about pluralism in the next chapter. What is important here is that the first shift required for a genuinely "open Catholicism" (in Rahner's phrase), a Catholicism that is no threat whatsoever to Jews or to other religious "neighbors," involves what is believed and proclaimed about Jesus. An initial stab at that shift occurred, in fact, not long after Anselm had constructed his theology of Jesus as the universal source of salvation. Indeed, Anselm was rebutted almost at once by Peter Abelard (1079–1142), another great theological figure of the time. He is remembered now more as the doomed lover of Héloïse (and, as always, a negative sexuality shaped Church attitudes there, too), but he embodies the hope that still adheres in Catholic theology. At issue between him and Anselm was the question of whether salvation was what Jesus came for in the first place. Salvation, as we just saw, is the solution to the hopeless divide between Creator and creatures, but Abelard, the author of *Sic et Non* (*Yes and No*), was not readily given to such discontinuities. For him, the natural world and, more to the point, the natural power of reason were occasions of connection with God, not division from God. The coming of Jesus was for the purpose of revelation, not salvation—revelation, that is, that we are all already saved. Creatures are saved not by virtue of the loving act of Jesus but by virtue of God's prior and constant love. The love of Jesus was "exemplary," a manifestation of God's love.

If this is so, then respect for human beings follows, whether they associate themselves with Jesus or not. As Genesis declares, God looked at everything God had made and saw that it was very good. That goodness remains, and so does God's unconditional positive regard for it. God loves the people no matter who they are, what they believe, or how they worship. Or, as Jesus himself put it, God "makes his sun rise on the evil and on the good, and sends rain on the just and on the unjust."[17] And recall that, for Jesus, being good or just was not a matter of being a believer but of caring for the neighbor. There is no ontological difference between the evil and the good, nor is there, with God, a hierarchy of the loved.

All that exists, and in particular all persons who exist, participate, by virtue of mere existence, in the existence of God. There is no question here of an unbridgeable gulf between the human and the divine. Christian Platonism yields to biblical faith. In this view, the Creation, more than salvation, is the pivotal event of being and of history, because the Creation is nothing less than God's self-expression. As Rahner explained, "God does not merely create something other than himself—he also gives himself to this other. The world receives God, the Infinite and the ineffable mystery, to such an extent that he himself becomes its innermost life."[18] Human beings are the creatures who instinctively respond to that innermost life. "This mystery," Rahner writes, "is the inexplicit and unexpressed horizon which always encircles and upholds the small area of our everyday experience . . . We call this God . . . However hard and unsatisfactory it may be to interpret the deepest and most fundamental experience at the very bottom of our being, man does experience in his innermost history that this silent, infinitely distant holy mystery, which continually recalls him to the limits of his finitude and lays bare his guilt yet *bids him approach;* the mystery enfolds him in an ultimate and radical love which commends itself to him as salvation and as the real meaning of his existence."[19]

For Christians, Jesus Christ is a revelation of that mystery. But Jesus did not come to put a fence around it, defining the corral gate as the way to salvation. There are numerous revelations of the mystery of God, and Vatican III will bring about a shift from, at most, a grudging tolerance of other religions to an authentic respect for other religions as true expressions of God "beckoning" the human heart.

Yet we saw that there was a kind of corralling of the meaning of Jesus when Hellenistic philosophical categories were pressed into service to explain it. The same would be true today, of course, if the new Christology were a product only of a reinterpretation in terms of the philosophical categories that have currency now. The most obvious such approach would take its cues from, say, the language philosophy of Wittgenstein, the existentialism of Kierkegaard, or the political gravity of Marxism. The theological preoccupation with hermeneutics, which gives me my interest in social and political context; my preference, in defining Christ's purpose, for the "subjectivity" of a change in human knowing over the "objectivity" of a change in the structure of the cosmos—these are manifestations of current philosophical assumptions. Nevertheless, the emphasis I am giving to Jesus the Revealer as opposed to Jesus the Savior—giving, that is, to Jesus as the "expressive Being" of God, to cite the term the Anglican theologian John Macquarrie uses[20]—is rooted in the Christian tradition. Indeed, my call for a revised Christology comes from within the countermemory of the tradition itself.

Moreover, the retrieval of a Christology that does not assume anti-Judaism for its other side requires a careful measuring of every affirmation about Jesus against what can be known of his life as a faithful Jew. The categories of philosophy, however instructive, are not enough to tell us who Jesus was—and they never were. In Anselm's schema, as in Nicaea's for that matter, the Jewishness of Jesus was lost, and so was the context of Israel's hope, apart from which Jesus can have no meaning. This is the essential part of what Vatican III must retrieve with its new Christology. It is impossible to understand the disclosure Jesus offers without knowing that the One being disclosed is none other than the God of Israel. Likewise, the suffering and death of Jesus must resume its place along the continuum of his entire experience. If the death of Jesus is no longer seen as the trigger of a transformation of a wrathful God, then the false idea of "the Jews" as perpetrators of that death will cease to have weight—then and only then. That is why the cross must be reimagined, and deemphasized, as a Christian symbol.

A new Christology, faithfully based in the Scriptures and available from a tradition that includes an Abelard, will in no way support supersessionism. It will in no way support a distrust of the body or a puritanical suspicion of sexuality or an ideology that puts males above females. A new Christology will banish from Christian faith the blasphemy that God wills the suffering of God's beloved ones, and the inhuman idea that anyone's death can be the fulfillment of a plan of God's.

Equally important, a new Christology, celebrating a Jesus whose saving act is the disclosure of the divine love available to all, will enable the Church at last to embrace a pluralism of belief and worship, of religion and no-religion, that honors God by defining God as beyond every human effort to express God.

In Rahner's image, God is the horizon, equally bidding all people to approach, yet equally distant from all people, Christians included. Vatican III will thus return to Jesus by returning to Rabbi Heschel and his liberating affirmation: "God is greater than religion . . . faith is greater than dogma."

6

Reform Proposal 4:
The Holiness of Democracy

M Y DEAR FELLOW CITIZENS, for forty years on
this day you heard from my predecessors the
same thing in a number of variations: how our
country is flourishing, how many millions of
tons of steel we produce, how happy we all are, how we trust
our government, and what bright prospects lie ahead of us. I assume you did not propose me for this office so that I, too,
should lie to you."

So began the address with which the playwright and dissi-
dent Václav Havel assumed the presidency of Czechoslovakia.
The speech was delivered on the first day of 1990. The momentous events of the previous months in the nations of eastern
Europe, symbolized by the breaching of the Berlin Wall in November 1989,[1] had amounted to an unpredicted outbreak of
democratic fervor. As Havel put it, "Humanistic and democratic traditions, about which there had been so much idle talk,
did after all slumber in the subconscious of our nations and national minorities."[2] In that period, the social structures of totalitarianism were transformed not only in the satellite states of
the Soviet Union but in Russia itself, not only in Europe but in

South Africa. And the dramatic changes came about almost completely without blood in the streets, because the masses of ordinary people in many nations discovered within themselves an irresistible civic identification, an urge to participate in the public life of society, a readiness to claim those nations as their own.

Citizens of the nations of western Europe and the United States, where democratic traditions were already established, could only behold the political transformations of the Velvet Revolution with an unbridled sense of wonder. What we saw played out again and again in those years, often with staggering courage — Havel declining a strings-attached release from prison, Lech Walesa openly convening meetings of the outlawed Solidarity movement in Poland, Boris Yeltsin standing on a Russian tank, saying, in effect, You will have to kill me first — was the drama of democracy itself, entire peoples taking responsibility for themselves and their societies. We in the West had never before seen so clearly how the political system under which we lived, and which we took for granted, counted as a moral absolute. Democracy was a value of the highest order, and the impulse to embrace it, at great cost, lived unquenchably in the human heart. In 1989, the world beheld something sacred, and the business of a new Vatican Council must be to honor that sacredness. Vatican III must end the Church's tradition of opposition to, or at best ambivalence toward, democracy. Vatican III must, that is, celebrate the dignity of every human life, uphold the importance of treating each one equally. Vatican III must affirm the holiness of democracy.

To their everlasting credit, the Christian churches of Europe supported, and in some instances sponsored, the 1980s flowering of the democratic spirit. The churches were especially helpful in keeping violence at bay. Lutheran pastors in East Germany played crucial roles in challenging the German Democratic Republic. And the Catholic Church, especially in Poland, was a source of spiritual, and at times political, inspiration and sustenance to the dissidents. Pope John Paul II was himself an avatar of anti-Communist resistance. His biographers uniformly credit him, sometimes with Ronald Reagan, as the man who did the most to bring down the totalitarian system he had opposed from his youth in Kraków.

Opposition to Stalinism is not the same thing as support for the principles of constitutional democracy, however, and the Roman Catholic Church has yet to shed its suspicion of, and even its hostility to, governments that invest the people with ultimacy — or rather, governments in which the people do the investing. This has been especially true in the Vatican's suppression of liberation theology, which is a religious affirmation of the political ideal of rights for all. Thus, in opposing Soviet totalitarianism, the Church nevertheless maintained its internal commitment to methods that undergird totalitarianism, which was why, even as the Soviet system crumbled, the Church was doing its part to shore up Latin American oligarchies.

The same John Paul II who sponsored the most politically engaged Church of modern times in Poland, to the extent of funneling large sums of money from the Vatican to Solidarity, condemned, silenced, and disciplined priests and nuns in Nicaragua, El Salvador, Guatemala, Brazil, Haiti, and Mexico because of their so-called political activity. The pope who wants to make Pius XII a saint is reticent about Oscar Romero, the bishop of El Salvador who was slain at the altar. The pope who railed against the ruthless dictators of Communism was the first and only head of state in the world to recognize the legitimacy of the military junta that overthrew the democratically elected president of Haiti (and former priest) Jean-Bertrand Aristide.[3] I say "so-called political activity" because the priests and nuns of the liberation insisted that their actions had more to do with their reading of the Gospel than any political tract. Observers of the difference between responses by the Catholic hierarchy in, say, Poland, where the Church lent support to Solidarity, and in Nicaragua, where the Church was a putative channel for money from the CIA during Ronald Reagan's Contra war,[4] were left with the feeling that it wasn't totalitarianism as such that the Church opposed, only totalitarianism that was unfriendly to the Church.

It was one thing for Pope Innocent III to declare the Magna Carta null and void in 1215 because it violated the divinely instituted order of hierarchy, and quite another for the Vatican, in its *instrumentum laboris* for the European synod of 1999, to equate pluralism with Marxism. It is impossible to reconcile a rejection of pluralism with an authentic commitment to democracy, and a Catholic devotion to the eradication of pluralism remains dangerous. Internal Church policies have relevance here because the use of anathemas, bannings, and excommunications to enforce a rigidly controlled intellectual discipline in the Church reveals an institution that has yet to come to terms with such ideas as freedom of conscience and the dialectical nature of rational inquiry.

The very idea of constitutional democracy begins with the insight that government exists to protect the *interior* freedom of citizens to be different from one another, and to cling, if they choose, to opposite notions of the truth. The political implementation of this insight requires a separation of church and state, since the state's purpose is to shield the citizen's conscience from impositions by any religious entity. And, of course, it tells us everything that this *political* insight was spawned, in the sixteenth and seventeenth centuries, by *religious* conflicts. As the forces of "secular enlightenment" targeted religion itself as the source of conflict, the Catholic Church understandably came vigorously to the defense of religion. Alas, the absolutism of the ensuing argument corrupted truth on both sides. The Church, for example, repudiated the violence of the Inquisition, but it continued to hold to the ideas that had produced it. The panic-stricken Vatican's sequence of condemnations in the nineteenth century—socialism, Communism, rationalism, pantheism, subjectivism, modernism, even "Americanism"—added up to a resolute denunciation of everything we mean by democracy. From the standpoint of the hill overlooking the Tiber, all of this was simply an effort to defend the key idea that the worlds of science, culture, politics, and secular learning were apparently conspiring to attack—the idea that there is one objective and absolute truth, and that its custodian is the Church.

The Church's rigidity during that period of conflict, from the Inquisition on, was central to what Pope John Paul II apologized for in his momentous declaration of March 2000. That apology was the beginning of a process, not the completion of one, because, while John Paul II confessed the sin of "the use of violence that some have resorted to in the service of truth,"[5] the apology did not confront the implications of that still maintained idea of truth. Universalist claims for Jesus as the embodiment of the one objective and absolute truth, launched from the battlement-like pulpits of basilicas, have landed explosively in the streets for centuries. Nothing demonstrates the links joining philosophical assumptions, esoteric theology, and political conflict better than the course of the story of Christology that we traced in the previous chapter. The violence of the heresy hunts of the fourth and fifth centuries is tied to that story, and so, at its other end, is the violence of Europe's imperialist colonizers who, even into the twentieth century, felt free to decimate native populations—"poor devils"—because they were heathens. Hanging from the line joining those two posts, in addition to the Inquisition, are the religious wars waged in the name of Jesus, not only against heathens and Jews, but against other Christians who believed, but wrongly.

Underlying all this is a question that Vatican III must confront, a question the answer to which shapes attitudes toward democracy and has profound relevance to the Church's past and future relations with the Jews. It is a question the answer to which shapes the meaning of Judaism's notions of monotheism, election, and chosenness, as well as of the Church's self-understanding as, in Rahner's phrase, the "absolute religion." It is the question that was put most famously by Pontius Pilate, in the Pilate-exonerating Gospel of John. This was an instant before Pilate told the Jews that Jesus was innocent, preparing the ground for Judaism's permanent blood guilt. "Everyone who is of the truth hears my voice," Jesus had just told Pilate. To which the Roman replied, "What is truth?"[6]

Classical philosophers had long answered that question by appealing to an objective and external order. We have seen that the various traditions claiming Plato and Aristotle as patrons had given shape to Christian theologies. The dualism of Christian Platonism posited a divide between nature and grace, with grace the realm of truth approachable only through faith. The more rationalistic tradition of Thomas Aquinas affirmed the compatibility of nature and grace, the knowability of God through reason. But in asserting the absolute character of truth, Thomas took note of the problem that occurs when a contingent, nature-bound creature attempts to perceive it. Truth, he said, is perceived in the mode of the perceiver. Human perception can take in the absolute truth, but not absolutely. Thus Thomas makes a modest claim for human knowing, with room for ambiguity—which means room for diverse claims made in the name of truth. Alas, this aspect of Thomas Aquinas's subtlety would be lost in the rigidities of the Catholic response to the Reformation.

René Descartes's *Discourse on Method* (1637) asserted that truth can be arrived at only on the basis of what is immediately self-evident, which eliminates knowledge gained through the unreliable senses. Therefore it is impossible to really know the truth—an impossibility that condemns the human mind to skepticism. It is this skepticism that the Catholic scholastics of the eighteenth and nineteenth centuries went to war against, and though they wrapped themselves in the mantle of Thomas Aquinas, calling themselves Thomists, they narrowly defined truth as the unambiguous conformity of the mind to the objective truth, without any sense that ambiguity might be a property of that mind. Enlightenment science had adopted a mechanical view of the universe that eliminated God (Nietzsche's *Thus Spake Zarathustra* announced the death of God in 1883). Ironically, to defend God the Thomists assumed an equally mechanical view of the universe, with a gear-like correspondence between nature and grace, subject and object, mind and truth. Imprecision, ambiguity, paradox, doubt, and mystery had as little place in the mind of a Catholic scholastic as in the mind of a catalogue-obsessed nineteenth-century naturalist.

Both are instances of what the Jesuit philosopher William

Lynch calls the "univocal mind." A univocal word has only one meaning, and a univocal community has only one voice. "The basic drive behind the univocal mind," Lynch wrote, "is the tendency to reduce everything, every difference and particularity in images, to the unity of a sameness which destroys or eliminates the variety and detail of existence."[7] This Catholic view of truth meshed perfectly with, indeed required, the nineteenth-century view of Catholic authority, whose role was to guard against ambiguity—which it could do, after 1870, infallibly. Once the Church, in its hierarchy, and in particular in the pope, had defined the objective truth, the duty of the Catholic was univocally to conform his or her mind to that truth.

But history has a way of challenging such ideas. The implications of Darwin's theory of evolution outran its first adherents and soon frustrated the most compulsive cataloguer. Human knowing is as dynamic as the development of species is. The absolute truth can in no way evolve or change (God as the Unmoved Mover), but what if everything else does? Then, in 1918, Albert Einstein published *Relativity: The Special and General Theory,* suggesting that neither the ground on which one stands while thinking nor the time in which one pursues a thought to its conclusion is free of ambiguity, paradox, contradiction, movement—relativity. Suddenly thinkers had a new language, based in physical observation, with which to describe the fact that every perception occurs from a particular point of view and that not even the point of view is constant. Every person is a perceiving center, and every perception is different. There is no strict conformity of the knowing subject to the known object. Therefore truth can be known only obliquely, and, yes, subjectively.

Change is built into the way truth is perceived, and every

person's perception has something to offer every other's. Therefore revision, criticism, dialogue, and conversation are far more relevant to truth-seeking than conformity to dictation from above. This flies in the face not of Catholic tradition but of *recent* Catholic tradition. For example, this existentialist framework fulfills the apophatic impulse of a great theologian and cardinal of the Renaissance, Nicolaus of Cusa (1401–1464). His *Learned Ignorance* (1440), affirming that God, and therefore truth, can be approached only indirectly, set the stage for his celebration of pluralism, *Peace Among the Religions* (1453), which was a call addressed to his *own* religion to abandon absolute truth-claims in the name of God. Unfortunately, Nicolaus of Cusa stood by another of those roads not taken.

Catholic theology spent much of the twentieth century recovering from the defensive rigidities of Counter-Reformation scholasticism, but the recovery is not complete. Vatican III must retrieve for the Church the deep-seated human intuition that mystery is at the core of existence, that truth is elusive, that God is greater than religion. "The heart of the matter is mystery in any religion," David Tracy said. "The Law is there for the Jew to intensify that sense of mystery, not to replace it. The Church is there for the Catholic to do the same."[8] If mystery is at the core of religion, then ambiguity, paradox, and even doubt are not enemies of faith, but aspects of it.

This is what Abelard saw, and Nicolaus of Cusa, and John Henry Newman, for whom the truth was like a tapestry, but seen from the reverse side, with all the imprecision that implies. Newman, who, after the fact, assented as an obedient Catholic to the infallibility decree he had opposed, nevertheless insisted that the nature of truth required modesty toward oneself and respect toward all others. "He was capable of holding a position," as the theologian Gerald Bednar observes, "while at the same time admitting the validity of a system very different from his own."[9]

But how? Are we condemned to a mindless pluralism that is ready to equate the shallow with the profound, the stupid with the wise, the cruel with the kind, all to avoid the monotony of the "one voice," the tyranny of the univocal? Does subjectivity condemn the person to the tyranny of the self? Does subjectivity condemn the community to, in David Tracy's phrase, "the void of sheer fascination at our pluralistic possibilities"?[10] Fearing the answer to those questions had to be yes, the Church set itself against democracy, and still openly regards pluralism with suspicion. But Lynch, Tracy, and others suggest that the antidote to the equivocation of modern skepticism is not the univocal but the "analogical imagination," which, in its approach to truth, as Lynch puts it, "insists on keeping the same and the different, the idea and the detail, tightly interlocked in the one imaginative act." Instead of a dualistic universe, with nature and grace impossibly alienated, or forced into the mold of one or the other, the analogical imagination posits a world in which every affirmation contains its own "difference, without ever suffering the loss of its own identity."[11] Difference, therefore, is to be respected, not condemned.

This idea, rebutting the excommunicating either-or of scholasticism, returns us to the both-and mind of Abelard, whose *Sic et Non* affirmed doubt and ambiguity as essential to the theological method. It is instructive to note that Abelard stood apart from his peers in his positive regard for Jews and other non-Christians, as reflected in his *Dialogue of a Philosopher with a Jew and a Christian.* Alas, he too stood by a road not taken, but, with Nicolaus of Cusa, he lives on in the memory of the Church as a reminder that the road is still there.

Tracy explains the vivid connection between such a frame of mind and the respect for a formerly hated other: "We understand one another, if at all, only through analogies. Each recognizes that any attempt to reduce the authentic otherness of another's focus to one's own with our common habits of domination only seems to destroy us all, only increases the leveling power of the all-too-common denominators making no one at home. Conflict is our actuality. Conversation is our hope."[12]

Conversation is our hope. In that simple statement lies the kernel of democracy, which is based not on *diktat* but on the interchange of mutuality. The clearest example of conversation as the sine qua non of democracy is the electoral process, in which candidates literally engage in conversation with the citizenry, opening themselves so that voters can judge them, but also changing their minds in response to interaction with the public. The proliferation of town meetings and debates in recent American political campaigns exemplifies this social equality and supports it.

There is a special tragedy in the fact that, for contingent historical reasons, the Catholic Church set itself so ferociously against the coming of democracy — tragic because Christianity began its life as a small gathering of Jews who were devoted to conversation. This was, of course, characteristically Jewish, since Judaism was a religion of the Book. Indeed, that was what made Judaism unique. That the Book was at the center of this group's identity meant that the group was never more itself than when reading and responding to texts, and while the rabbinical schools may have presided over the process, all Jews participated in it, especially after the liturgical cult of sacrifice was lost when the Temple was destroyed. Gatherings around the

Book became everything. Conversation became everything. The assumption among the followers of Jesus was that they were all endowed with the wisdom, insight, maturity, and holiness necessary to contribute to the pursuit of the truth of who Jesus had been to them.

The religious language for this assumption had it that all believers were endowed with the Holy Spirit, which was seen to reside in the Church not through an ordained hierarchy but through all. That is why the apostolic writings are nothing if not manifestations of pluralism. Indeed, there are four Gospels, not one. Each has its slant, and each slant, in this community, has its place. "That there is real diversity in the New Testament should be clear to any reader of the text," David Tracy comments, and he goes on to note that the first Christians could admit the validity of positions not their own — from the charismatics to the apocalyptics to the zealots to the prophets.[13] There is even a diversity of images that disclose the meaning of Jesus' life, with some giving emphasis to the ministry, some to the death, some to the symbolic assault on the Temple, some to the expected return. There are those who emphasize bringing the Gospel to the Gentiles and those who insist on the Gospel's place within the hope of Israel. And because the texts gather all of this, honor it, and declare it *all* sacred, nothing could be further from the mind of the early Church than making its subjects conform to a narrowly defined "objective truth." The Spirit was seen to be living in all, and the truth, for all, remained shrouded in mystery.

It would be anachronistic, of course, to read this as evidence of an early Church polity that was what we would call democracy. That does not mean, however, that democracy, by taking each member of the community as of ultimate worth, equal to every other, is not a fulfillment of the biblical vision that attributes just such valuing of each person to God. Isaac Hecker, the American who founded the Paulist Fathers, argued that America and Catholicism were inherently compatible because of this. To Hecker, the equal rights of citizenship were a secular expression of the religious "indwelling of the Spirit" in each person. When this idea was brought to Europe at the end of the nineteenth century, Leo XIII condemned it as the heresy "Americanism." In particular, the pope denounced the idea "that certain liberties ought to be introduced into the church so that, limiting the exercise and vigilance of its powers, each one of the faithful may act more freely in pursuance of his own natural bent and capacity."[14] The anathemas were nearly pronounced over Hecker himself. My own life as a twentieth-century Catholic, in dissent from a nineteenth-century Catholicism, began with my falling under Hecker's spell. Vatican III should rescind the condemnation of "Americanism," acknowledging that the "pursuit of happiness" assumes the "pursuance" of one's natural bent and capacity, and that nothing better defines the purpose for which our Creator made us.

So the answer to Pilate's question, What is truth?, matters. If truth is the exclusive province of authority, then the duty of the people is to conform to it. That answer to the question fits with the politics of a command society, whether a monarchy, a dictatorship, or the present Catholic Church. But if truth is, by definition, available to human beings only in partial ways; if we know more by analogies than syllogisms; if, that is, we "see in a mirror dimly,"[15] then the responsibility of each person is to bring one's own experience and one's own thought to the place where the community has its conversations, to offer and accept criticism, to honor the positions of others, and to respect oneself, not in isolation but in this creative mutuality. The mutuality, in this community, has a name: the Holy Spirit.

The implication here is that truth is not the highest value for us, because, in Saint Paul's phrase, "our knowledge is imperfect and our prophecy is imperfect."[16] Which is why the final revelation of Jesus is not about knowing but about loving. This, too, places him firmly in the tradition of Israel, which has always given primacy to right action. "Beloved," the author of the First Epistle of John wrote, "let us love one another; for love is of God, and he who loves is born of God and knows God. He who does not love does not know God; for God is love." This statement of a biblical faith in the ultimate meaning of existence *as love* is a classic affirmation of what one might call the pluralistic principle: respect for the radically other begins with God's respect for the world, which is radically other from God. In other words, God is the first pluralist. "In this the love of God was made manifest among us, that God sent his only Son into the world, so that we might live through him. In this is love, not that we loved God but that he loved us and sent his Son to be the expiation for our sins. Beloved, if God so loved us, we also ought to love one another. No man has ever seen God; if we love one another, God abides in us and his love is perfected in us."[17]

Religious pluralism begins with this acknowledgment of the universal impossibility of direct knowledge of God. The immediate consequence of this universal unknowing is that we should regard each other respectfully and lovingly. But our clear statement of Christian openness to the other is its own revelation. The epistle just cited is attributed to John, the author of the fourth Gospel. It was apparently written about the same time as the Gospel, around the turn of the first century. It was addressed to Christian communities that were riven with disputes that had arisen after the destruction of the Temple and at the time of the first serious conflict between what was becoming known as the Church and the Synagogue. This plea, whatever else it referred to, concerned the tragedy then beginning to unfold—it is John whose Gospel demonizes "the Jews" above all. And the tragedy is underscored by the fact that in this same letter John, as if understanding already what is at stake in the conflict, begs his readers to "not be like Cain who was of the evil one and murdered his brother. And why did he murder him? Because his own deeds were evil and his brother's righteous."[18] The tragedy, and the sin, and what must forever warn us off cheap talk of love, is that all too soon, and all too easily, the followers of Jesus were content to read these words and identify Cain with Jews.

That sin, embedded in the Gospel itself, is proof of why the Church needs democracy, for the assumption of democratic politics, in addition to the assumption that all citizens can contribute to the truth-seeking conversation, is that all citizens are by nature incapable of consistent truth-seeking and steadfast loving. God may be love, but the *polis* isn't, and neither is the Church. The language of love is often used by those in power, while the language of justice is used by those who suffer from the abuse of power. The language of love is not enough, because it does not protect us from our failures to love; only the language of justice does that.

Democracy assumes that a clear-headed assessment of the flaws of members extends to everyone. But even the leaders of democracies, especially in the United States, salt their speeches with Christian chauvinism or an excluding religiosity, assuming that a democratic polity could be called univocal—no voices, that is, for religious minorities or those of no religion. And that, finally, is why a democracy assumes that everyone must be protected from the unchecked, uncriticized, and unregulated power of every other, including the well-meaning leader. The universal experience of imperfection, finitude, and self-centeredness is the pessimistic ground of democratic hope. The Church's own experience—its grievous sin in relation to the Jews, and lately the inability of clerical leaders to dismantle an autocratic structure that enabled priestly child abuse—proves how desperately in need of democratic reform the Church is.

Vatican III must therefore turn the Church away from autocracy and toward democracy, as the Catholic people have in fact already done. The increased grassroots participation by lay people in changing the Church is a first step. Vatican III must solidify this impulse and restore the broken authority of the Church by locating that authority where it belongs, with the people through whom the Spirit breathes.

Vatican III must affirm that democracy is a gift from a God who operates in history, and the only way for the Church to affirm democracy is by embracing it. The old dispute between popes and kings over who appoints bishops was resolved in favor of the pope, but bishops now should be chosen by the people they serve. The clerical caste, a vestige of the medieval court, should be eliminated. Vatican III must establish equal rights for women in every sphere. The Church must institute a system of checks and balances, due process, legislative norms designed to assure equality for all instead of superiority for some, freedom of expression, and above all freedom of conscience. The long and sorry story of Church hatred of Jews and the fresh outrage of child abuse both lay bare the structures of oppression that must be dismantled once and for all.

7

Reform Proposal 5: Repentance

P**ULL OUT HIS EYES**," the children chant in the mind of Stephen Dedalus. "Apologise, / Apologise, / Pull out his eyes."[1] The impulse by public figures to apologize has come to be distrusted, because words are cheap and apology has become an arrow in the well-equipped politician's quiver. An American president apologizes to Africans for failing to stop a genocide, while the United States, the richest nation in the world, ranks ninth in the percentage of national wealth given to combat worldwide AIDS, which kills more Africans than all the continent's wars put together. British Prime Minister Tony Blair acknowledges the failure of "those who governed in London at the time" to avert the famine known to the Irish as the Great Hunger, but Blair was hooted at by Ulster Unionists who said, "The Irish mentality is one of victimhood—and to ask for one apology one week, and another on a different subject the next."[2] The Vatican issues "We Remember: A Reflection on the Shoah" as an "act of repentance," yet puts responsibility for failure on the Church's children, not the Church; it never mentions the Inquisition, and it praises the diplomacy of Pius XII. John Paul II offers a millennial mea culpa early in the year 2000, and while there was a profound significance in that apology as far as it went, it revealed how far is the distance that must be traveled yet. And in June 2002, Bishop Wilton D. Gregory, president of the U.S. Conference of Catholic Bishops, offered an apology on the bishops' behalf, despite the fact that he presided over the Dallas meeting that never took up the question of the bishops' own responsibility for the sex abuse crisis. Indeed, several bishops have apologized profusely, with little apparent inclination to attack the clerical culture that is the obvious problem.

As the document "Memory and Reconciliation" put it, "Memory becomes capable of giving rise to a new future."[3] But the current leadership of the Church seems interested only in partial memory and a limited reckoning with the past, whether the issue is antisemitism or clericalism. Otherwise John Paul II would not have devoted so much of his papacy to maintaining the very modes of thought and governance that were the historic sources of Church failure. Apologies offered too glibly, in other words, can be a sly way of asserting one's own moral superiority while reifying the victim status of the group to whom apologies are offered. This is especially so if the structures of that victimization remain in place.

"When Willy Brandt fell on his knees on the site of the Warsaw ghetto in 1970," the scholar Ian Buruma has written, "it was a moving and necessary acknowledgment of a great crime. But such symbolic gestures are too precious to become routine. Official tears have become too cheap, too ritualistic. Piety is often a substitute for knowledge and understanding."[4] Knowledge and understanding should be our purpose, and the next council will accomplish nothing if it falls back, as the Church has so often done, on piety. But something else seems possible now, in the aftermath of John Paul II's millennial call for "the purifica-tion of memory."

That is more than a matter of mere words. Far more impor-tant than uttered apology, for example, was his momentous act in Israel only two weeks after the liturgy of repentance, an event that transcended the routine symbolic gestures of which Bu-ruma warns. In Jerusalem in April 2000, John Paul II left his wheeled conveyance to walk haltingly across the vast plaza be-fore the Western Wall. For two thousand years, beginning with the Gospels, Christian theology has depended on the destruc-tion of the Temple as a proof for claims made in the name of Jesus, the new Temple. Nothing signifies Christian anti-Judaism more than this attachment to the Temple in ruins, which prompted the pagan emperor Julian to order it rebuilt in the fourth century, and which reinforced Vatican ambivalence to-ward the state of Israel in the twentieth. So when John Paul II devotedly approached the last vestige of that Temple, and when he placed in a crevice of that wall a piece of paper containing words from his previously offered prayer for forgiveness — "We are deeply saddened by the behavior of those who in the course of history have caused these children of yours to suffer" — more than an apology occurred.

Though the news media missed its significance, this moment outweighed the pope's later, emotional visit to Yad Vashem, the Holocaust memorial. By bending in prayer at the Western Wall, the Kotel, the pope symbolically created a new future. The Church was honoring the Temple it had denigrated. It was af-firming the presence of the Jewish people at home in Jerusalem. The pope reversed an ancient current of Jew hatred with that act, and the Church's relationship to Israel, present as well as past, would never be the same. Referring to the sight of the stooped man in white with his trembling hand on the sacred stones of the wall, a senior Israeli official said, "This is a picture that will appear in the history books—both Catholic and Jewish."[5]

An authentic confrontation with history results in the opposite of self-exoneration. That is why the members of Vatican III, in taking up repentance as an agenda item, must do so only after having confronted the questions embedded in revelations tied to the Church's absolutism and the consequent questions of fundamentalist readings of texts, power, Christology, and democracy, all of which point to attitudes and structures of triumphalism that must be uprooted if the Church is truly going to turn toward other believers and its own people with a new face. Again, reflection on the legacy of antisemitism is particularly instructive. Remorse over the silence of the Church in the face of the Shoah—the *faute* to which the French bishops confessed in 1997—is not enough. Neither is guilt over the ways two millennia of Church antisemitism prepared for the Shoah.

Authentic repentance presumes what we Catholics used to call "a firm purpose of amendment," which Jews call "desisting" from what led to sin.[6] Simply put, repentance presumes change—at every level of the Church's life, because it is at every level that the poison of antisemitism has had its effect. *Teshuva* is the word Jews use to describe the process by which repentance and forgiveness take place. The word means "return," and here is Rabbi David R. Blumenthal's summary of what *teshuva*, in this context, implies: "All the words, documents, and genuine expressions of contrition will avail naught without concrete actions . . . The way the Church deals with terrorist incidents, antisemitism, Church files on the period of the Shoah, Judaica deposited with various Church entities and not returned, Catholic education about Jews and Judaism, the nature of Catholic mission, relations with the State of Israel, relations with local Jewish communities everywhere, etc., are, thus, the action-yardsticks by which Catholic teshuva is measured."[7] Such changes — education, mission, relations — require the changes in doctrine and structure I have indicated. I call for those changes as a Catholic, but in fact I am following, as David Tracy put it, "Jewish theology [which], in its reflections on the reality of God since the *Tremendum* of the Holocaust, has led the way for all serious theological reflection."[8]

And so with every manifestation of the Church's need for reform. There can be no deflection, whether thinking of pogroms or of clerical child abuse, from the deeper problems of context and culture that spawn such sins, and there must be no more talk that exempts the "Church as such" from full moral reckoning. Instead, with Karl Rahner, who wrote generally of the "sinful Church of sinners," the confession must be made that the failures that brought Catholicism to the present crisis are "the actions and conduct of the Church herself."[9] The culture of the Church itself — its clericalism, triumphalism, absolutism — must be renounced, as the culture that has kept the structure of victimization of the other so firmly in place, even now.

If the next reforming council is held in the Vatican, its members would have to face the moral challenge of the Catholic masterpiece in the Sistine Chapel, *The Last Judgment*. That painting was the greatest achievement of the greatest genius who ever worked for the Church, Michelangelo.

To enter the chapel, with its remarkable frescoes on the ceiling and walls, is to enter a jewel box. The cardinals of the Church have long met here to elect the pope, an act of historical continuity. Yet the huge painting behind the high altar, toward which the room is oriented, portrays nothing less than the end of history.

Michelangelo was an old man when he mounted the scaffolding to paint this last great work, and you can see how time had flogged him. He had created the serenely poignant *Pietà* as a young man in 1499, but since then Luther, Copernicus, Magellan, Henry VIII, and several Borgia popes had all helped to upend the moral universe. The grand inquisitor Gian Pietro Caraffa had come to Rome, and soon, as Pope Paul IV, would establish the Roman ghetto, which popes would maintain until the late nineteenth century. *The Last Judgment,* painted between 1534 and 1541, reflects the era's loss of faith in the human project, and it is a window into Michelangelo's soul. His scathing vision is staggering, especially because it so contrasts with the earlier hopefulness of the scenes on the ceiling just above, with their triumphal rendition of the Creation. *The Last Judgment,* as it were, rebukes *The Creation,* for the beautiful creature to whom God had entrusted the spark of divinity, with that unforgettably outstretched finger, is now repudiated. Sinners and the righteous alike cower below the upright figure of the judging Lord. It is as if Michelangelo, looking afresh into the soul of humanity, had glimpsed the coming religious wars, slavery, Inquisition, genocide, death camps, and the Church's betrayal of its own children.

To me, the most heart-rending and fearsome aspect of Michelangelo's dark masterpiece is not despair overtaking the created world, but a smaller and more personal statement. Among the multitude of figures in *The Last Judgment* is a rare Michelangelo self-portrait. It is so discreetly done that his contemporaries failed to see it as him, and no wonder. Michelangelo, the genius celebrant of the human body, the creator of *David* and *Moses* and the *Pietà,* chose to put his own face on a shriveled, limp, formless skin that had been flayed from the body of a martyr.[10] Apparently the artist had lost all sense of the noble things he had done and was still doing. The self-portrait of a face ripped from its bones is an abject confession of sin, impossible to behold out from under the crushing weight of conscience. The portrait says, "I stand as accused by God as anyone in this scene." As the artist who conjured the devastating judgment of his own era, Michelangelo is saying, through his portrait, "There is nothing of which I accuse any other person here — popes, Borgias, Medicis — that I do not accuse myself of."

"You have utterly betrayed me," one hears the damning Lord declare — and what Catholic can imagine hearing such words today without shuddering? *Woe to him,* Jesus declared in Luke, as if foreseeing through the centuries this very Church catastrophe. "It would be better for him to be thrown into the sea with a millstone around his neck than he should lead astray any one of these little ones!"[11]

But *The Last Judgment* is not thereby a *Catholic* vision or even a Christian one. It is biblical faith that is fully in touch with the mystery of evil as it lurks in the human heart, and it is biblical faith that includes, always, the call to judgment. In the supersessionist rewriting of biblical narrative, the judging God stands in contrast to the redeeming God of the New Testament, but that is a total fabrication, unfaithful to the history of Israel and the story of Jesus. Despite the darkness with which Michelangelo renders it, judgment is the opposite of despair. Judgment, which is "action revealing itself fully," in Hannah Arendt's phrase, is the source of meaning. That is why visitors to the Sistine Chapel, after marveling at the grandeur of the

Creation scene above, stand transfixed before the fresco on the wall behind the altar.

What do they see? In the burly nakedness of the majestically centered Christ figure, whose right arm is raised above his head, poised for one cannot say what, the doomed and the saved equally search for, in Arendt's phrase, "the possible redemption from the predicament of irreversibility—of being unable to undo what one has done though one did not, and could not, have known what he was doing." If the past is irreversible, then we are all doomed. No one can be saved. Is the history of Christian anti-Judaism reversible? Can the Church recover from the sin of sexual self-hatred? These are far more potent questions than Are such sins forgivable? But only apparently so. For as Arendt goes on to say, "Forgiving serves to undo the deeds of the past, whose 'sins' hang like Damocles' sword over every new generation ... Without being forgiven, released from the consequences of what we have done, our capacity to act would, as it were, be confined to one single deed from which we could never recover; we would remain the victim of its consequences forever."[12]

Arendt is not talking here about the easy forgiveness disparaged above, nor, in the context of the ancient crime of anti-semitism, does forgiveness like this necessarily come from Jews, any more than it necessarily comes from victims of clerical child abuse. For both Jews and abuse victims, forgiveness may equate with denial. The premature request for forgiveness, made by a Christian to a Jew or by an abuser to a victim, may constitute presumption at best, a further oppression at worst. That is why the acts of repentance offered by a council of the Church must carry no hint of a required or expected response, as if victims, however defined, have to accept it for the act to be complete. But there is another problem. The political philosopher Emmanuel Levinas, among others, has warned that the erasure of the past through cheap forgiveness, whereby the soul can "free itself from what has been," can slide all too easily into a valueless individualism according to which "no attachment is ultimately definitive."[13]

In Arendt's view, the human disposition to seek forgiveness, which responds to the otherwise irreversible predicament of the past, is protected from presumption and from irresponsibility when it is paired with the quest for a "remedy for unpredictability, for the chaotic uncertainty of the future, [which] is contained in the faculty to make and keep promises." In other words, there is no recovery from the past without a commitment for the future. More concretely, there is no apology for Holy Week preaching that prompted pogroms until Holy Week liturgies, sermons, and readings have been purged of the anti-Jewish slanders that sent the mobs rushing out of church. There is no apology for sexual abuse or denigration of women, too, until the theologies that lead to such sins are fully repudiated. Here is the core meaning of reform and the urgency of it. Without reform, repentance is impossible, and so is recovery.

The capacity to be forgiven resides in the simultaneous capacity to make and keep a promise that "serves to set up in the ocean of uncertainty, which the future is by definition, islands of security without which not even continuity, let alone durability of any kind, would be possible in the relationships between men."[14] The Church, in other words, must be an island of security for Jews, women, children, homosexuals, and all others who are vulnerable to the abuse of power. We saw in the previous chapters what this means for the institution of the Church.

What does it mean for us as individuals? To be suspended

between past and future, in Arendt's phrase, is to stand between the world into which our beloved parents brought us and the world to which we are sending our beloved children. How do we get out from under the irreversibility of our past, which is another way of asking, How do we get out from under the sword of self-doubt? How is the chaotic uncertainty of the future to be tamed? The most deadly prospect at this point would be to find ourselves alienated from the community that has been the focus of our call for reform. Instead of issuing the call from the position of moral purity we may once have imagined ourselves occupying, haven't we felt flayed by every word? Like Michelangelo, don't we find ourselves unable to accuse our Church of any sin that we cannot equally accuse ourselves of?

The act of reflecting on all that history requires of the Catholic Church has left us readier than ever before to claim membership in this community, if only because we recognize ourselves in all of those who have failed. "Do we really have the right to cast the first stone at the sinful woman who stands accused before the Lord and is called the Church," Rahner asks, "or are we now accused in her and with her, and delivered up to Mercy for good or ill?"[15] It is only through this communion of saints and sinners that we have our connection to the biblical people for whom judgment, forgiveness, and the promise-making of covenant are all the same thing. And as Arendt writes, "No one can forgive himself and no one can feel bound by a promise made only to himself; forgiving and promising enacted in solitude or isolation remain without reality and can signify no more than a role played before one's self."[16] Therefore, one dares to join in the call for Catholic reform as a way both of making the necessary promise and of hoping to be forgiven.

That fuller meaning of the word "promise," implying our

grave obligation as well as our hope, governs the subtitle of this book, "The Promise of Reform."

Participants in Vatican III will be aware of Peter as the patron of the imperial basilica and as the avatar of papal domination. Yet always Peter is something else. We may hope the participants keep in their thoughts the story of Simon Peter spying a stranger on the beach. It is some days after the death of Jesus, the one whom this Peter betrayed not once but three times. Simon Peter is in his fishing boat with the others. They have worked through the night. In the haze of dawn, he watches the figure on the beach. The boat draws closer to shore. The figure is bent over a fire, preparing a meal. When Peter steps from the boat and approaches the man, he seems familiar. The meal is the first hint. The second is the act of judgment, for this stranger faces Peter with the truth of his condition as fiercely as the Christ of Michelangelo will the human world with the truth of its condition. The irreversible act that stands between these two is betrayal. Peter had loved Jesus, but also, three times—"and at once the cock crowed"[17]—he denied him.

Here is the real power of the Church's ancient association of itself, centrally, with Peter—not that he was a rock of virtue, not that his authority was absolute, but that his failure of the Lord was so complete. Peter at its mythic center—this is how the Church defines itself as a Church of sinners and betrayers: the cowardly Church, which has so often put power over service; the threatened Church, which has used its old feud with the Jewish people to wall itself off from the fear that its faith in Jesus is misplaced. As the story of Jewish-Christian conflict renders undeniable, the Church, having betrayed Jesus in its first generation, has been betraying Jesus ever since, as clerical abuse victims make clear once again. That a flawed Peter is the patron saint of this Church is the principle of its self-criticism.

For each time that Peter denied Jesus, the figure shrouded in the haze of dawn puts to him the question "Simon Peter, do you love me?" And each time, Peter replies, "Yes, Lord, I love you."

Then, "Feed my sheep."[18] Three times the figure calls Peter to this service. The threefold betrayal is reversed by a threefold ritual of forgiveness, built upon a promise.

That meals and feeding are central to this story, that the mysterious figure of Jesus is recognized in the breaking of bread, gives shape to the Catholic faith. It is in attending Mass, partaking of the meal as one of a number of people who are almost always strangers to us, that we draw near to the figure whom we recognize. His story is ours, and we have it through the Church. Human history is a story told by God, and by attending to history, even tragic history, we draw near to God. Reform is always necessary and always possible, which is what this history tells us. And it is what the Mass affirms, which is why we go to the table so often. At the offertory of the Mass we hand over to God, especially, the ones we love. We confess our sin—the sin of the Church—three times. And three times we hear the word of hope. The Eucharistic bread keeps us alive, and we believe it always will.

Notes

Epigraph

Quoted by Peter Hebblethwaite, *Pope John XXIII: Shepherd of the Modern World* (Garden City, N.Y.: Doubleday, 1985), 499.

1. What Is to Be Done?

What Is to Be Done? is the title of a novel by the Russian social reformer N. G. Chernyshevsky, published in 1863. In 1902 Lenin used the same title: *What Is to Be Done? Burning Questions of Our Movement.*

1. Karl Rahner, S.J., *Theological Investigations*, vol. 5, *Later Writings*, translated by Karl-H. Kruger (London: Darton, Longman and Todd, 1975), 116–17.

2. Diana Eck, *A New Religious America* (San Francisco: HarperSanFrancisco, 2001), 3.

3. Hans Küng, *Judaism*, translated by John Bowden (New York: Crossroad, 1992), title page.

4. *Boston Globe*, January 6, 2002, A1.

5. Ibid.

6. Investigative Staff of the *Boston Globe, Betrayal: The Crisis in the Catholic Church* (New York: Little, Brown, 2002), 96.

7. For an illuminating analysis of Church dishonesty, see Garry Wills, *Papal Sin: Structures of Deceit* (New York: Doubleday, 2000).

8. "The attitudes of that body [the bishops] regarding crime and punishment are so far from being representative even of the views of Catholics that they are currently the object of intense national (and entirely ecumenical) criticism." "Scalia Comment Questions Bishops," *Boston Globe,* June 22, 2002, A4.

9. "As Lawsuits Spread, Church Faces Questions on Finances," *New York Times,* June 13, 2002, A1.

10. The president of Voice of the Faithful, Dr. James Muller, told me this at a meeting in Boston on June 10, 2001.

11. *New York Times,* May 31, 2001, A17.

12. For an example of prelates holding "the Church as such" to be the sinless Bride of Christ, see "We Remember: A Reflection on the Shoah," www.jcrelations.net/stmnts/vatican3-98.htm.

13. "I will betroth you to myself forever ... It is Yahweh who speaks." Hosea 2:21–22.

14. I acknowledge Robert Kuttner, whose use of this traditional blessing in a poem inspires my use of it. Robert Kuttner and Sharland Trotter, *Family Re-union* (New York: Free Press, 2002), 235.

2. The Broad Relevance of Catholic Reform

1. I wrote about this encounter in *An American Requiem* (Boston: Houghton Mifflin, 1996), 76–79.

2. "The often so misanthropic and bureaucratic Church must die," Hans Küng wrote, "and the philanthropic Church of Jesus must again and again resurrect in our hearts." Küng, *Reforming the Church Today,* translated by Peter Heinegg et al. (Edinburgh: T. & T. Clark, 1992), 163.

3. Quoted by Peter Hebblethwaite, "John XXIII," in *The Harper-Collins Encyclopedia of Catholicism,* Richard P. McBrien, general editor (San Francisco: HarperSanFrancisco, 1995), 709.

4. "I am not infallible," John XXIII said. "The pope is infallible only when he speaks *ex cathedra.* But I will never speak *ex cathedra.*" Quoted by Küng, *Reforming the Church Today,* 69.

5. Hebblethwaite, "John XXIII," 710.

6. John XXIII, *Pacem in Terris,* in David J. O'Brien and Thomas A. Shannon, eds., *Renewing the Earth: Catholic Documents on Peace, Justice, and Liberation* (Garden City, N.Y.: Image Books, 1977), 134.

7. Quoted by Hebblethwaite, "John XXIII," 709.

8. Küng, *Reforming the Church Today,* 66–67.

9. Reinhard Neudecker, S.J., "The Catholic Church and the Jewish People," in *Vatican II: Assessment and Perspectives,* vol. 3, edited by René Latourelle (New York: Paulist Press, 1989), 283.

10. Hannah Arendt, *Men in Dark Times* (New York: Harcourt, Brace and World, 1968), 63.

11. Neudecker, "The Catholic Church and the Jewish People," 283.

12. Küng, *Reforming the Church Today,* 65.

13. For an analysis of the "structure of deceit" tied to the Church's position on birth control, see Garry Wills, *Papal Sin: Structures of Deceit* (New York: Doubleday, 2000), 78–79. The contemporary rejection of Church authority on this and other issues has been a definitive turn in the Catholic story. For example, here are the percentages by which American Catholics dissent from Church teaching: on birth control, 93%; divorce, 85%; abortion, 69%; homosexuality, 51%; women's ordination, 60%. See Alan Wolfe, "Liberalism and Catholicism," *American Prospect,* January 31, 2000, 20.

14. "And all the people answered, 'His blood be on us and on our children!'" Matthew 27:26.

15. Quoted by Neudecker, "The Catholic Church and the Jewish People," 288.

16. Ibid., 286.

17. Ibid., 282–83.

18. Quoted by John W. O'Malley, *Trent and All That* (Cambridge: Harvard University Press, 1993), 18.

19. Hans Küng, *The Council, Reform, and Reunion,* translated by Cecily Hastings (New York: Sheed and Ward, 1961), 9–10.

20. Quoted by John T. Ford, "Infallibility," *The HarperCollins Encyclo-*

pedia of Catholicism, Richard P. McBrien, general editor (San Francisco: HarperSanFrancisco, 1995).

21. Hans Küng, *Infallible? An Unresolved Enquiry*, translated by John Bowden (New York: Continuum, 1994), 77.

22. Michael Burns, *Dreyfus: A Family Affair* (New York: Harper-Perennial, 1992), 50.

23. *Pastor Aeternus*, in Henry Edward, Archbishop of Westminster, *The Vatican Decrees in Their Bearing on Civil Allegiance* (New York: Harper and Brothers, 1875), 154–55. See also Küng, *Infallible?*, 77.

24. Hans Kühner, *Encyclopedia of the Papacy* (New York: Philosophical Library, 1958), 229.

25. Ford, "Infallibility," 664.

26. Quoted by Roland Hill, "'I Am the Tradition': How the Pope Became Infallible," *Times Literary Supplement*, no. 5009 (April 2, 1999), 9.

27. *Pastor Aeternus*, in Edward, *Vatican Decrees*, 167.

28. Ibid., 159–60.

29. Gregory XVI, quoted in *National Catholic Reporter*, December 11, 1998.

30. Alan Wolfe, "Liberalism and Catholicism," *American Prospect*, January 31, 2000, 16–21.

31. Quoted by Küng, *The Council, Reform, and Reunion*, 162.

32. In this context, Hans Küng recalls Voltaire, but also Dante, who placed three popes in hell (Ibid., 46). Küng is the greatest contemporary advocate of Catholic reform, but he remains a fiercely committed Roman Catholic. The Vatican, under John Paul II, tried to silence him in 1979, particularly because of his questioning of papal infallibility, but Küng has refused to be silent. He has refused to leave the Church. His case has special poignancy for Catholics because his 1961 book, *The Council, Reform, and Reunion*, gave expression to a generation's hope for Vatican II. He has suffered the consequences of the Church's failure to fulfill that hope.

3. Reform Proposal 1: A New Biblical Literacy

1. Hans Küng, *Reforming the Church Today,* translated by Peter Heinegg et al. (Edinburgh: T. & T. Clark, 1992), 160. A step toward such a lifting of the anathema was taken in the 1999 Joint Declaration on the Doctrine of Justification, issued by the Lutheran World Federation and the Vatican. This statement represented a mutual acknowledgment by the former antagonists that each side had its point.

2. Küng, *The Council, Reform, and Reunion,* 74.

3. Joyce Carol Oates, "The Calendar's New Clothes," *New York Times,* December 30, 1999.

4. Luke 24:25.

5. John 1:11.

6. John 8:23, 40–44.

7. See Nancy Levine, ed., "Teaching Troubling Texts," *Textual Reasoning* 8, no. 2 (November 1999), 1.

8. The phrase is Christopher Leighton's, quoted by Padraic O'Hare, *The Enduring Covenant* (Valley Forge, Pa.: Trinity Press International, 1977), 9.

9. See, for example, Eugene J. Fisher, *Seminary Education and Christian-Jewish Relations* (Washington, D.C.: National Catholic Educational Association, 1988); Phillip A. Cunningham, *Education for Shalom* (Collegeville, Minn.: Liturgical Press, 1995).

10. Krister Stendahl, *Paul among Jews and Gentiles, and Other Essays* (Philadelphia: Fortress Press, 1976). See also Stendahl, *Final Account: Paul's Letter to the Romans* (Minneapolis: Fortress Press, 1995), 1–7, 35–40.

11. Romans 11:1.

12. Luke 22:20.

13. Jeremiah 31:31–34. What the Revised Standard Version translates as "new covenant" carries the sense, in Hebrew, of "renewed."

14. Norbert Lohfink, S.J., *The Covenant Never Revoked,* translated by John J. Scullion (New York: Paulist Press, 1991), 83. Paul van Buren, a Christian leader in the Jewish-Christian dialogue, ap-

proached the problem this way: "As for ourselves, the Gentile Church, I believe that we are the fruit of one of the many renewals of the one covenant. It turned out strangely, but then so have many other creative renewals of that covenant. This particular renewal led to a new entity called the Church, consisting of Gentiles mostly, who found in one Jew an opening to the knowledge and love of the God of the covenant, and a calling to serve that God in a Gentile way. It is a tragedy of major proportions that we failed for so long to see that this was the universal God's particular calling for us, alongside Israel's particular calling. If we are beginning to see that now, it is because Christians have begun in the last couple of decades finally to meet Jews and so discover a living covenant." Van Buren, "When Christians Meet Jews," in Eugene J. Fisher, ed., *Visions of the Other* (New York: Paulist Press, 1994), 65.

15. David Tracy, *The Analogical Imagination* (New York: Crossroad, 1981), 426.

16. Gregory Baum, introduction to Rosemary Radford Ruether, *Faith and Fratricide* (New York: Seabury, 1974), 17–18.

17. Robert Nozick, *Philosophical Explanations* (Cambridge: Harvard University Press, 1981), 597n.

18. Some scholars already routinely refer to "Hebrew Scriptures" and "Christian Scriptures" as a way of avoiding the Old Testament–New Testament dichotomy, but this division suggests that the Hebrew Scriptures are not part of what Christians revere. Another formulation, "First Testament" and "Second Testament," seems off too. "Apostolic Writings" is also used to define the specifically Christian texts.

19. In a session devoted to "troubling texts" at a meeting of the American Association of Religion in Boston, November 1999, I heard Professor Robert Goldenberg say, "Troubling texts are only truly troubling if the tradition is *not* troubled by them . . . An ethical act of reading requires a reading as if you are the Jew, the woman, the Canaanite. Then the glory of the texts is their troubling character."

20. David Tracy, *On Naming the Present* (Maryknoll, N.Y.: Orbis Books, 1994), 14.

21. David Hartman, "Judaism Encounters Christianity Anew," in Eugene J. Fisher, ed., *Visions of the Other* (New York: Paulist Press, 1994), 76–77, 79.

4. Reform Proposal 2: The Church and Power

1. Quoted by Jaroslav Pelikan, *Jesus Through the Centuries* (New Haven: Yale University Press, 1985), 108.

2. John Paul II, "Universal Prayer: Confession of Sins and Asking for Forgiveness," March 12, 2000, www.jcrelations.net/stmnts/vatican3-00.htm.

3. Elisabeth Schüssler Fiorenza and David Tracy, "The Holocaust as Interruption and the Christian Return to History," *Concilium,* October 1984, 86.

4. Elisabeth Schüssler Fiorenza, *In Memory of Her* (New York: Crossroad, 1989), xiv.

5. See Garry Wills, *Papal Sin: Structures of Deceit* (New York: Doubleday, 2000), 2.

6. Quoted by Eugene Kennedy, "A Dissenting Voice: Catholic Theologian David Tracy," *New York Times Magazine,* November 9, 1986, 28.

7. Quoted by Hans Küng, *Reforming the Church Today,* translated by Peter Heinegg et al. (Edinburgh: T. & T. Clark, 1992), 157.

8. Ibid., 156.

9. Rosemary Radford Ruether, *Faith and Fratricide* (New York: Seabury, 1974), 245.

10. David Tracy, *On Naming the Present* (Maryknoll, N.Y.: Orbis Books, 1994), 14–15.

11. Hans Küng made this point in conversation with me. See James Carroll, "The Silence," *The New Yorker,* April 7, 1997, 60.

5. Reform Proposal 3: A New Christology

1. Abraham Joshua Heschel, *The Insecurity of Freedom* (Philadelphia: Jewish Publication Society, 1966), 119.
2. Rosemary Radford Ruether, *Faith and Fratricide* (New York: Seabury, 1974), 246.
3. David Tracy, *Dialogue with the Other* (Grand Rapids, Mich.: Eerdmans, 1991), 98.
4. Genesis 1:27.
5. Elizabeth A. Johnson, "Jesus and Salvation," *CTSA Proceedings* 49 (1994), 5.
6. "Homily at Auschwitz, June 7, 1979," in John Paul II, *Spiritual Pilgrimage: Texts on Jews and Judaism, 1979–1995*, edited by Eugene J. Fisher and Leon Klenicki (New York: Crossroad / Anti-Defamation League, 1995), 7.
7. John 6:63.
8. Karl Rahner, S.J., *Theological Investigations*, vol. 5, *Later Writings*, translated by Karl-H. Kruger (London: Darton, Longman and Todd, 1975), 120.
9. Cardinal Joseph Ratzinger, "Universal Prayer: Confession of Sins and Asking for Forgiveness," March 12, 2000, www.jcrelations. net/stmnts/vatican3-00.htm.
10. Thomas F. O'Meara, in *The HarperCollins Encyclopedia of Catholicism*, Richard P. McBrien, general editor (San Francisco: HarperSanFrancisco, 1995), 1077.
11. Rahner, *Theological Investigations*, vol. 5, 116–17.
12. Numerous theologians have developed versions of this "anonymous Christianity," all seeking to protect the universalist claims for Jesus Christ. Raimon Panikkar, for example, speaks of "the Unknown Christ of Hinduism." For a discussion of the possibilities and limits of these approaches, see Jacques Dupuis, *Toward a Christian Theology of Religious Pluralism* (Maryknoll, N.Y.: Orbis Books, 1997).
13. Rahner, *Theological Investigations*, vol. 5, 116.
14. Quoted by John L. Allen, Jr., "Doubts about Dialogue: Encounter

with Other Religions Runs Up Against the Vatican's Hard Doctrinal Realities," *National Catholic Reporter,* August 27, 1999.

15. After a storm of protest greeted the Vatican's action, particularly from Balasuriya's fellow theologians, he was reinstated as a member of the Church, though he refused to recant his theological positions.

16. www.vatican.va/roman_curia/congreg . . . cfaith_doc_20000806-_dominus-iesus_en.html.

17. Matthew 5:45.

18. Rahner, *Theological Investigations,* vol. 5, 171–72.

19. Karl Rahner, S.J., *The Rahner Reader,* edited by Gerald McCool (New York: Seabury, 1975), 20.

20. John Macquarrie, *Principles of Christian Theology* (New York: Scribner, 1966), 183.

6. Reform Proposal 4: The Holiness of Democracy

1. Curiously enough, the wall was breached on November 9, the anniversary of Kristallnacht. Because of the overwhelming significance of the dismantling of the wall, that anniversary trumped the earlier one in the German, and European, memory. This is a prime example of supersessionism.

2. "Playwright-Dissident Václav Havel Assumes the Presidency of Czechoslovakia," in *Lend Me Your Ears: Great Speeches in History,* selected and introduced by William Safire (New York: Norton, 1992), 629, 631.

3. Monsignor Lorenzo Baldisseri presented his diplomatic credentials as papal nuncio to the junta in Port-au-Prince on March 30, 1992, six months after the overthrow of Aristide. No other nation followed suit, and eventually, after an American invasion in 1994, Aristide was restored to the presidency.

4. Jonathan Kwitny, *Man of the Century* (New York: Henry Holt, 1997), 467.

5. John Paul II, homily, St. Peter's Basilica, March 12, 2000.

6. John 18:37–38.

7. William F. Lynch, S.J., *Christ and Apollo* (New York: New American Library, 1963), 118.

8. David Tracy, quoted by Eugene Kennedy, "A Dissenting Voice: Catholic Theologian David Tracy," *New York Times Magazine,* November 9, 1986, 28.

9. Gerald J. Bednar, *Faith as Imagination* (Kansas City: Sheed and Ward, 1996), 16f.

10. David Tracy, *The Analogical Imagination* (New York: Crossroad, 1981), 362.

11. Lynch, *Christ and Apollo,* 136.

12. Tracy, *The Analogical Imagination,* 363.

13. Ibid., 252.

14. Quoted by David J. O'Brien, *The Renewal of American Catholicism* (New York: Paulist Press, 1972), 106–7.

15. 1 Corinthians 13:12.

16. 1 Corinthians 13:9.

17. 1 John 4:7–12.

18. 1 John 3:12–13.

7. Reform Proposal 5: Repentance

1. James Joyce, *A Portrait of the Artist as a Young Man* (New York: Viking, 1960), 8.

2. Quoted by Sarah Hall, "Past as Prologue: Blair Faults Britain in Irish Potato Blight," *New York Times,* June 3, 1997.

3. "Memory and Reconciliation: The Church and the Faults of the Past," www.jcrelations.net/stmnts/vatican12-99.htm, 4.1.

4. Ian Buruma, "War Guilt and the Difference Between Germany and Japan," *New York Times,* December 29, 1998. Buruma is the author of *The Wages of Guilt: Memories of War in Germany and Japan* (New York: Farrar, Straus and Giroux, 1994). In December 1999, the president of Germany, Johannes Rau, said, "I pay tribute to all those who were subjected to slave and forced labor under German rule and, in the name of the German people, beg for-

giveness." But this was said at a private observance. A month later, at ceremonies dedicating the site for a Holocaust memorial near the Brandenburg Gate in Berlin, Elie Wiesel urged the German parliament to "do it publicly. Ask the Jewish people to forgive Germany for what the Third Reich had done in Germany's name. Do it, and the significance of this day will acquire a higher level. Do it, for we desperately want to have hope for this new century." Quoted by Roger Cohen, "Wiesel Urges Germany to Ask Forgiveness," *New York Times,* January 28, 2000.

5. Quoted by Ben Lynfield, "For Israelis, Papal Visit Struck a Deep Chord," *National Catholic Reporter,* April 7, 2000.

6. David R. Blumenthal, "Repentance and Forgiveness," *Cross Currents* 48 (Spring 1998), 76.

7. Ibid., 81.

8. Quoted by John T. Pawlikowski, O.S.M., "Christian Theological Concerns after the Holocaust," in Eugene J. Fisher, ed., *Visions of the Other* (New York: Paulist Press, 1994), 32.

9. Karl Rahner, S.J., *Theological Investigations,* vol. 5, *Later Writings,* translated by Karl-H. Kruger (London: Darton, Longman and Todd, 1975), 15–16. Rahner goes on to say, "It would be silly self-deceit and clerical pride, group-egoism and cult of personality as found in totalitarian systems — which does not become the Church as the congregation of Jesus, the meek and humble of Heart — if it were to deny all this, or tried to hush it up or to minimize it, or made out that this burden was merely the burden of the Church of previous ages which has now been taken from her."

10. H. W. Janson, *History of Art* (New York: Abrams, 1986), 454.

11. Luke 1:1–3.

12. Hannah Arendt, *The Human Condition* (Chicago: University of Chicago Press, 1958), 236–37.

13. Quoted by Tina Chanter, "Neither Materialism Nor Idealism: Levinas's Third Way," in Alan Milchman and Alan Rosenberg, eds., *Postmodernism and the Holocaust* (Amsterdam, Netherlands: Rodopi, 1998), 143.

14. Arendt, *The Human Condition,* 237.
15. Rahner, *Theological Investigations,* vol. 5, 17.
16. Arendt, *The Human Condition,* 237.
17. John 18:27.
18. John 21:15–17.